THE RACE FOR THE
2012 OLYMPICS

THE RACE FOR THE
2012 OLYMPICS

The Inside Story of How
London Won the Bid

Mike Lee
with
Adrian Warner
David Bond

First published in Great Britain in 2006 by
Virgin Books Ltd
Thames Wharf Studios
Rainville Road
London
W6 9HA

A catalogue record for this book is available from the British
Library.

ISBN 0 7535 1152 5
ISBN 978 0 7535 1152 7

Typeset by TW Typesetting, Plymouth, Devon
Printed and bound in Great Britain by
CPD Wales

The paper used in this book is a natural, recyclable product made
from wood grown in sustainable forests. The manufacturing
process conforms to the regulations of the country of origin.

Dedication
To my family, Heather, Alex and Euan
– their support got me to the finishing line.

CONTENTS

Adrian Warner, the *London Evening Standard* Sports News Correspondent, has regularly reported on the International Olympic Committee for a decade and has covered ten Olympic Games since 1988.

David Bond is a former Deputy Sports Editor of the *Evening Standard* who coordinated the paper's coverage of the London Olympic bid. The former *Sunday Times* writer recently joined the *Daily Telegraph*.

ACKNOWLEDGEMENTS

Trying to capture something as complex and lengthy as an Olympic bid campaign is not an easy task. This book is an attempt to tell the story of London's successful bid to host the 2012 Olympic and Paralympic Games by focusing on the highs and lows and the perceptions of some of the key players along the way.

The thread that draws it together is my own. In that sense it is my story. However London's success was a result of the Herculean efforts of so many. From the local communities of the East End of London to the tireless campaigning of the bid's supporters up and down the country, the London bid was won by people with commitment and belief.

Some are mentioned in the course of this book but most are not, such is the nature of book writing and story-telling.

For all those who gave so much I want to record the thanks of every member of the bid team. It was a great campaign and ultimately a tremendous victory for British sport and the country as a whole.

A number of bid colleagues and backers have helped me recapture the rollercoaster ride that was the London 2012 bid campaign. My thanks are due for their support and co-operation. Their names may well be familiar to readers (do read on) and I have tried to reflect the contribution they made to securing victory.

In writing the book I am hugely indebted to Adrian Warner and David Bond, two sports journalists with a real passion for Olympic sport, who have worked so hard to help me capture the amazing story of this particular Olympic race.

For all those who believed London could win and helped secure that victory – thank you. This story is for you.

Mike Lee, July 2006

FOREWORD

by Rt Hon. Tony Blair, Prime Minister

The final announcement of who was to host the 2012 Olympic and Paralympic Games was one of those moments when the whole country holds its collective breath.

I'll have to admit that I was so nervous that I went outside into the grounds of the Gleneagles hotel rather than wait to hear live the results of the final ballot.

So I actually learnt that London had won a few seconds after the rest of the world.

It didn't, however, stop me joining in the national celebrations. I am only glad there was no photographer around to record my jig of joy.

London's success was an extraordinary moment, made even sweeter because I knew both how incredibly hard Lord Coe and the whole team had worked and how fierce the competition had been.

London won, I believe, because we put together a superb, ambitious but practical bid that echoed strongly the ideals of the Olympic movement.

The focus on the power of sport to reach out and enthuse young people in Britain and across the world left a deep impression on the International Olympic Committee.

So, too, did the emphasis we put on ensuring the Games would leave a legacy of superb sporting facilities and transformed communities.

But the outcome was never a foregone conclusion. That made the final announcement even more memorable.

From the very beginning to that last nerve-tingling final ballot, London was never the favourite. In fact, if we had listened to some voices back home, we wouldn't have bothered putting in a bid at all.

The full story of how London came from behind to win this race is fascinating and instructive. It shows just what our country can achieve if we have confidence in ourselves.

Mike Lee was in the perfect place to tell the story with all its twists and turns. As Seb's communications chief and adviser, he was there every step of the way in the two-year campaign to bring the Games back to the UK.

In researching the book, Mike and his co-writers have spoken to all the key figures including Seb, London 2012 chief executive Sir Keith Mills, Olympics Minister Tessa Jowell, Sports Minister Richard Caborn, London Mayor Ken Livingstone, Britain's IOC member Sir Craig Reedie and many more people from the well-known to those unfamiliar outside the bid team itself. It was a real, fantastic collective effort.

He's spoken as well to Cherie and myself about our memories of meeting IOC delegates in Athens and Singapore in the tense days before the final ballots.

Winning the honour of hosting the Games is, of course, only the first stage. Now we have to deliver on our vision and ambition. I am confident we will.

I believe the 2012 Games in London will be both magical and memorable and will more than do justice to the great Olympic ideals.

It will be a national sporting festival, with teams from around the world preparing in towns and cities up and down the country and spectators visiting other Olympic-related events outside of London.

The Games will provide as well a fantastic opportunity to showcase modern Britain in all its diversity and dynamism and prove a catalyst for investment to improve life and health not just in East London but across the UK.

All this – the wonderful sporting memories and the tremendous legacy – are now within our grasp. This book reveals how we won the chance to host the greatest show on earth and what it will mean for this country. Enjoy.

FOREWORD
by Lord Coe

The abiding memory I have of the bid is of a hugely dedicated and highly committed team. Right from the very beginning when I walked into the bid's offices on the top floor of Canary Wharf tower I was struck by the energy and passion of a small knot of people perched on a cluster of chairs in the middle of a huge empty space. Barbara and the team literally started with nothing.

700 or so days later on the eve of our departure to Singapore Keith Mills and I gathered together the team, substantially larger by this time, to prepare them for the final push and to remind everyone these finals days in London and Singapore were the culmination of over two years of extraordinary work together. We were going into the final stage of our campaign in the best shape we could hope to be in thanks to the people around me. As I looked around at the faces in the room I could see the pride in every set of eyes that looked back at me. They all knew what it had taken to get to that day. They all knew that their part was an important part of a collective goal. They all knew they were part of an astonishing team and they all knew they could rely on each other to do their bit to get us across the line.

As a team our metal was probably best tested when the IOC Evaluation Team came to London. The level of detail and hours of rehearsal that went into every single aspect of that visit was outstanding. The late nights and very early mornings, the 'lost' weekends and cancelled holidays were the norm as individuals delivered the best they had to make the team effort that much stronger.

It is hard to describe the pride I felt during that visit. The exceptional quality of the presentations, the sheer scale, organisation and planning of the whole event, the presence of smiling team members and supporters as I escorted the IOC commission members around our venues, the branding of the city – night and day – and the careful management of the media. Watching the team over those few days probably held more emotion for me than the announcement in Singapore – and that is a pretty hard moment to beat! There is something incredibly powerful about watching a committed, focussed and exceptionally talented team working well together.

I learnt a lot about people in that time and I will carry with me the hard work, skill, expertise and humour that I was proud to be a part of.

Many of the great moments we shared as a team are recounted in Mike's book. It is his story of a journey that we took together as a team. Every setback was overcome by a collective approach to finding a solution, every victory along the way was won by a series of individual endeavours pulled together in a massive co-ordinated effort.

Much of what we are proudest of in life is achieved through teamwork.

I am often asked for my proudest achievement – winning Olympic Gold Medals or winning the 2012 Games? I am sure I have answered that question in many different ways but actually the one thing they both have in common is that they are both defined by the fact I was part of extraordinary teams. Neither endeavour would ever have been as successful without the team that supported it.

The Olympic Games changed my life. The 2012 Olympic and Paralympic Games will change the lives of many more people. It will act as an enormous catalyst for change and regeneration in the East End of London and will inspire young people in the UK and around the world to take up sport and embrace the Olympic ideals. This will be an enduring legacy and one that each member of the bid can feel proud of.

I cannot thank the London 2012 bid team and all our supporters enough and I hope they each find some memories in Mike's story that will remind them of the extraordinary journey we took together, memories that I hope will bind us all together for always.

Lord Coe, July 2006

PROLOGUE – ONE SWEET WORD

On 6 July 2005 at 7.46 p.m. Singapore time, Jacques Rogge, President of the International Olympic Committee took an agonising twenty seconds to tear open the envelope containing the name of the city which had won the vote to host the 2012 Games. I would never have believed that in this age of mobile phones, email and the BlackBerry, the opening of a good old-fashioned envelope could still be such a dramatic, life-changing event. My nervous apprehension had reached fever pitch as I, and of course, millions of people around the world, watched and listened.

London and Paris had reached a showdown in the last round of voting, and now, in those two great cities (huge crowds had assembled at Trafalgar Square and at the Hôtel de Ville) countless thousands were gathered around television sets, or following events on the radio or internet.

Most of the British public watched the television pictures from Singapore's Raffles Hotel more in hope than with any real expectation of success. Many feared the frantic lobbying in the final 72 hours before the IOC vote would not be enough, despite the fact that Prime Minister Tony Blair, bid chairman, Sebastian Coe, and the London 2012 team had done everything they could to secure victory.

Paris had been the favourite for the two years of campaigning and the bookmakers were expecting a French victory. Paris appeared to have it all – an Olympic stadium already built, excellent contacts within the IOC and enthusiastic public support for the campaign.

The French crowd that gathered outside the magnificent Hôtel de Ville in Paris watching the TV pictures on a large screen was noisily confident. They believed that, after two previous failed bids for the 1992 and 2008 Games, the International Olympic Committee members would not turn their backs on Paris for a third time.

Clearly, the media in the Raffles Hotel expected a Parisian triumph – all the photographers were lined up opposite the French delegation, ready to shoot pictures of celebration. As the IOC President took the piece of card from the envelope, one French TV commentator told the nation: 'This is perhaps an historic hour for Paris.' He paused as Rogge, the 63-year-old former Olympic yachtsman, began reading the card in front of him. From Singapore to Trafalgar Square everyone held their breath.

The agonising wait was finally over in the time it took to say 23 words: 'The International Olympic Committee has the honour of announcing that the Games of the thirtieth Olympiad are awarded to the city of . . . London.'

This was a historic moment. In years to come Britons will still remember where they were when they heard the news. Across London and Britain, a nation famous for its modesty and reserve, clapped and cheered, while those watching at home whooped in front of their TV sets, as veteran BBC commentator Barry Davies shouted: 'We've done it! London has won it! Absolutely brilliant!'

I am happy to say that I was in the thick of the wild celebrations in the Raffles ballroom in Singapore, hugging and kissing the colleagues with whom I had worked many long days, as London 2012's communications director and Seb Coe's special adviser.

But I did not have long to savour the moment. Now that we had won the bid, I had to tear myself away to start arranging the interviews for Seb with reporters from national and international television, radio and newspapers.

After a few precious minutes of unbridled exuberance, I had to face once again the logistical challenges of dealing with the media. Even now it is hard to describe how I felt as the enormity of London's victory began to sink in.

I walked away from the celebrations wondering at the events that had led to this glorious moment.

This was a bid that was on its knees in the spring and summer of 2004, when anybody suggesting London would beat Paris would have been laughed out of court.

London's bid for the 2012 Olympic and Paralympic Games had been controversial from the moment of its conception, in the offices of the British Olympic Association in the late 1990s, to the final days of campaigning in Singapore. Before the bid could even be put before the International Olympic Committee it had taken every ounce of persuasion to rally support for the idea from a sceptical Cabinet, a critical general public and a cynical press.

London's victory in Singapore was simply one of the most remarkable results in the history of Olympic bidding. So how did a bid, so unpromising less than a year before the vote, end up beating the favourite Paris in this dramatic Singapore finale? How did London produce one of the most astonishing comebacks in Olympic history?

Seb Coe and I exchanged a wry smile as we left the Raffles ballroom to face the waiting media. We knew the secrets of London's success.

Mike Lee, July 2006

1. FALSE STARTS

The Sydney Harbour Bridge exploded in a dizzying burst of colour as fireworks lit up the sky above the famous Opera House. It was a postcard scene which had been witnessed many times by millions of people around the world. But never before had it been seen like this. As the giant golden Olympic rings, which had sat proudly on the side of the bridge for the two-week duration of the 2000 Olympics, were switched off, Sydneysiders said farewell to the first Games of the new millennium in style. They had plenty to celebrate. Their Olympics had been an enormous triumph. After battling for so many years against a feeling that theirs was a forgotten continent, the Games they staged for the rest of the world that year gave all Australians an immense sense of pride. So, when International Olympic Committee (IOC) President Juan Antonio Samaranch declared Sydney's Games the best ever, for once you sensed he really meant it.

In Britain the impact was enormous. After the disappointing performances of the British team at the 1996 Atlanta Games where they won only one gold medal, the success in Sydney was a massive shot in the arm for British sport. In total Team GB won eleven golds and produced their best performance at a Games for eighty years. The fairytale rowing performance of Sir Steve Redgrave in the coxless four was the highlight. It confirmed the giant oarsman as the greatest British Olympian with five gold medals in consecutive Games. Back home the country had Olympic fever as millions tuned in despite the time difference to soak up the events unfolding down under. It was at this point that the dream of bringing the Olympics back to Britain really caught the public's imagination.

In fact Sydney played a more direct role in the country's eventual decision to bid for the 2012 Games than many people realise. For it was amid the ruins of Manchester's desperate failure to bring the 2000 Games to Britain that the realisation dawned on British Olympic chiefs they would only ever stand a chance of staging the Games if they bid with London. Manchester's second failure running had come as no surprise at the vote in 1993 in Monte Carlo. Sydney were shock winners but Manchester and Britain were never in the race. In the end Manchester polled just eleven votes. Simon Clegg, chief executive of the British Olympic Association (BOA), recalls: 'The very clear message was that only when we came back with London would the IOC believe we were serious about wanting to host the Olympic Games.'

But it was not until 1997 that the first serious steps were taken towards mounting a London bid. Clegg and the BOA appointed David Luckes, the goalkeeper from the Great Britain men's hockey team in Atlanta in 1996, to research a possible bid. Luckes, who was to subsequently play an important behind-the-scenes role in the London bid, undertook a feasibility study into the possibility of staging the Olympics in the capital. With no back-up staff and not even an office to call his own at the BOA's headquarters in Wandsworth, South London, Luckes began investigating whether a bid could work and whether it should be focused on the East End or West End of the city. 'I actually sat in the corridor for three or four months after I started,' Luckes said. 'But at least it allowed me to get to know most of the people in the building. I spent a long time looking at the bidding process and possible venues and whether London's transport infrastructure could cope with staging the Games. I looked at East London and West London alternatives and tried to put a proposal together which we could take out to the London boroughs and the government.'

By the time the Sydney Games had weaved its magical spell on the nation, Luckes had produced a 395-page report on the London Games. Although it offered a West London alternative, focused mainly on a redeveloped Wembley Stadium, the opportunity to regenerate the run-down East End of the capital was clearly more favourable. There were already plans to redevelop a vast corridor of wasteland from the Isle of Dogs in London's Docklands up through the East London area of Stratford and north into the Lower Lee Valley of North London and Hertfordshire. Adding the Olympic bid to that scheme made perfect sense. At last Britain had the basis of a potentially successful bid.

But establishing that London had the potential to bid was just the beginning of an even more tortuous journey. First the British Olympic Association had to wait to see which city would win the 2008 Games at the IOC Session in Moscow in July 2001. The Games are rarely held in the same area of the world two times running, historically moving between Europe, North America, Asia and Australasia. Although Beijing was the clear favourite, despite concerns over China's human rights record, Paris was strongly fancied as an outsider. Victory for the French would end any hopes London had of the Games coming to Europe in 2012. It would be 2016 at the earliest before London would get another chance. The land that had been earmarked by planners for a new Olympic Park in the East End would be sold and redeveloped for other uses by then and the opportunity would be lost, possibly forever. So it was a huge relief for those in support of the bid when Beijing stormed home comfortably.

London's backers were on a high and the campaign began to build some early momentum. Then, in the autumn, a potentially calamitous problem reared its head. In October 2001 Britain was forced to withdraw London's offer to stage the 2005 World Athletics Championships at a new purpose-built stadium in the heart of the Lee Valley, at Picketts Lock, in Hertfordshire.

Tessa Jowell, the incoming secretary of state for Culture, Media and Sport, anxious that lessons be learnt from the government's recent experiences of the Wembley Stadium project and the Millennium Dome, was concerned that the Picketts Lock proposal was unsound. She demanded a full report on the feasibility of the plan.

The subsequent report by Patrick Carter, a successful businessman and one of a number of leading entrepreneurs relied on by the New Labour government to advise ministers on major projects and policy decisions, confirmed serious questions about the viability of the Picketts Lock proposal. Carter's report stated that the transport infrastructure was inadequate and there were serious question marks over costs. Carter, who was later to become chairman of the sports lottery distributor Sport England, told Jowell that the plug had to be pulled. Jowell and her Sports Minister, the Sheffield MP Richard Caborn, duly obliged.

The decision sent shockwaves through world sport. Already under pressure because of the controversy over the £757 million Wembley redevelopment project and the much-publicised problems of the Dome, Britain's sporting reputation, on the international stage could not have been any worse. It was not helped when the government tried to persuade the President of the International Association of Athletics Federations (IAAF), Lamine Diack, that Sheffield could provide a viable alternative venue for the championships. Diack, also a member of the IOC, was not impressed and the event was moved to Helsinki.

Even if London could get a bid out of the starting blocks for 2012, critics believed the ill feeling created by the Picketts Lock débâcle would strangle London's hopes at birth. Despite the massive setback, however, the BOA refused to give up. Clegg and Luckes had already won the support of the Mayor of London, Ken Livingstone, provided the bid fulfilled his vision for transforming the desperately deprived East End and increased investment in the capital. Livingstone's support was a critical development and despite the Picketts Lock fiasco, Jowell and Caborn were convinced that the time was right to bid. To this day the government remains convinced that, had the World Athletics Championships come to London in 2005, they would have been a disaster. In the long run, ministers argue, Britain's reputation was better protected by the decision not to proceed particularly given the aversion to risk which had developed in the Cabinet following Wembley and the Dome.

To move forwards, consultancy specialists Arup were commissioned by the government to carry out a study on the London Olympics. Yet even as they crunched the numbers and explored where each of the Olympic sports could be staged in the capital, another potential dark cloud loomed large on the horizon – the 2002 Commonwealth Games in Manchester. Another sporting flop would mean the end for the London bid and confirmation of Britain's image as a nation incapable of hosting major sporting events. And for many months, with costs at the new City of Manchester Stadium soaring, it looked like this might happen. The government again sent for Patrick Carter. He moved quickly, ordering Manchester City Council to find the money to make the event work, and in August 2002 the Games were opened in spectacular style by the England football captain David Beckham. It had cost more than expected but the 'friendly Games', as they became known, were a huge triumph.

The IOC President, Jacques Rogge, and IAAF President Lamine Diack, both came to Manchester to witness the event first hand. Afterwards they spoke of their admiration for the show Britain had put on. The Picketts Lock, Wembley and Dome episodes could not be entirely forgotten but the British had shown they could throw a party for the world.

Suddenly it was all systems go for London. By the late autumn of 2002 Arup reported their findings back to the government. A small group of Cabinet ministers formed a special Olympic sub-committee, chaired by Foreign Secretary Jack Straw, to examine the details more closely, but it was clear that the government was a long way from being convinced. After five years of planning and lobbying, London's Olympic dream entered its most critical phase.

Arup's report predicted that the cost of the Games would be £1.8 billion, with the government having to stump up £484 million of that total bill. Arup also estimated that the London Olympics would generate £610 million in revenues and could end up making an operating surplus of £79 million. The report was a massive boost for the bid's backers who pointed out how favourably the Arup costings compared with the final bills for past Games.

The magnificent Sydney Games of 2000 had cost £1.9 billion while Atlanta four years earlier cost £1.8 billion.

However, the low price tag only served to make sceptical ministers even more cynical, believing the figures were not sustainable. While Prime Minister Tony Blair was thought to be broadly in favour of a bid provided it was winnable, there remained massive scepticism within his cabinet. Political heavyweights such as the Chancellor of the Exchequer Gordon Brown, Transport Secretary Alistair Darling, Deputy Prime Minister John Prescott and Jack Straw all needed to be convinced. They cited the problems of the Dome and pointed to the difficulties created by the new Wembley and Picketts Lock. They were concerned that another grand project could cost billions of pounds and possibly end up haunting them for the next decade. In fact, at this time Jowell and the Prime Minister were the only members of the Cabinet who truly believed the risk was worth the potential benefits of bringing the Olympics to London. And back in August, at the same time as the Commonwealth Games in Manchester were proving such a hit, Jowell had been advised to reject the idea of a London bid by her own officials.

A departmental report prepared by senior civil servants in the Department of Culture, Media and Sport warned her that it was not winnable and would cost too much money. But, enthused by the vision for the East End and the potential legacy for sport and for London, Jowell ignored the advice. Instead she spent the autumn re-analysing the costs and trying to persuade her Cabinet colleagues in a series of critical private meetings.

There was support from the Prime Minister, that was clear. In fact his wife Cherie was one of the project's early cheer-leaders. She undoubtedly played a key role in persuading her husband to get behind London. She explains: 'I thought it was fantastic. I was an athletics fan because my mum had been an athletics fan. We went to watch the Commonwealth Games in Edinburgh in 1986.

'Then of course I got really excited because we went to the Manchester Games, having missed the Sydney Olympics because my son Leo had just been born. But the Olympics were already a big part of my life.' At one stage Cherie Blair was even touted as a possible bid leader. But she says: 'The idea of me leading the bid was never a realistic prospect because it wouldn't have been appropriate but I could see the potential where I could help because of all the travel abroad and here.'

Despite the support from the Blairs, Jowell still faced a huge struggle to win the backing of the rest of the key players in government. 'I knew I had a massive job to persuade the Cabinet,' she explains, 'but after the Commonwealth Games and the Queen's Golden Jubilee celebrations, there was a much greater sense of confidence that we could organise things.

'Tony and Cherie Blair had both been at the Commonwealth Games and were very enthusiastic. Despite that I spent the autumn meeting other ministers and there was a tremendous amount of scepticism while at the same time the Iraq crisis was beginning to rumble and become a serious preoccupation for the government.'

Jowell was convinced that with time her colleagues could be won over, she says 'One of the things John Prescott said to me early on in the process was that if all the Cabinet were given sufficient time then they would come around to the idea. That was one of the big problems with the Dome – no one felt they had been given enough time to really look at the project properly.'

Gordon Brown, concerned about the prospect of a downturn in public spending, was the toughest person to convince but Alistair Darling was also worried the bid would distort his spending plans on transport. All were worried about the Dome effect and felt they had enough to deal with without taking on another risky scheme. Jowell recalls one story where one minister ended a meeting by telling her: 'I hope the Olympic Games are a huge success – in Paris!'

In an effort to ensure that the government was given all the facts, Jowell, ordered a review of the Arup report. Robert Raine, a senior civil servant who had worked for many years in the Cabinet Office, was asked to take a look at the costings. He had previously worked with Patrick Carter on the Wembley, Picketts Lock and Manchester Commonwealth Games reviews. On each occasion he found costs had been massively underestimated and his latest foray into the world of sport was to be no different.

What he found left many fearing the worst: Arup had underestimated the costs by a staggering £800 million. Raine found they had failed to factor in the costs of purchasing land, upgrading transport facilities, security, project risks and inflation. Of greatest concern, however, was the fact Arup had only allowed for £450 million of contingency costs to cover parts of the project when they went wrong. Raine believed that at least 10 per cent of the total budget needed to be factored in for this, 4 times more than Arup's estimate. Raine predicted the cost of staging the Games in London would be £2.4 billion. And that didn't even include the costs of improving London's creaking transport network. Arup protested that Raine had gone too far, citing the £100 million cost Raine had factored in for transport management. Arup's estimates were far more reliable, direct from the Metropolitan Police, which said the real total was nearer £20 million.

The BOA feared Brown and other senior ministers would order the London Games to be strangled by the Raine review. They were convinced that was the end of it. And as the 30 January date for a government decision drew nearer the debate continued as to whether it was right that such a vast sum of money should be used to pay for a month of sport. And if the Olympics went over budget who would pick up the tab?

Craig Reedie, the BOA chairman and British IOC member, watched the turn of events with growing trepidation. Reedie was the driving force behind the proposed London bid and believed the delay was threatening to wreck London's chances. Even if the government did decide to back the Games then it might still be too late to get everything in place in time to mount a serious challenge to Paris.

'We heard the rumours,' he says. 'It was a genuine fear that the Raine review was only implemented because the government wanted to kill the bid.

'Arup could have come up with the same figures as Robert Raine but they were told to factor in costs at 2002 levels. All

Raine did was factor in inflation up to 2012. It was designed to make it more expensive and all we asked for from government was consistency.

'We were very fearful but in a sense there was nothing I could do about it. I could not get any further up the tree than the Secretary of State for Culture, Tessa Jowell. She was on side and to that extent we were in her hands.'

The most critical week of the fledgling campaign began on Monday, 13 January 2003 and Jowell was at the centre of it. It started with a difficult meeting with the Chancellor. Citing fears over the costs, Brown told Jowell that he could not support the bid at this stage but remained open to persuasion as long as there was a much greater clarity on the finances.

The next day Jowell faced a grilling from a select committee of MPs chaired by the outspoken Manchester MP Gerald Kaufman, one of the government's arch critics on major sporting projects. Then later that same day she had to lead a debate on the London bid in the House of Commons. It was a delicate moment and with behind-the-scenes private meetings continuing, Jowell did not want to get ahead of the Cabinet. She felt unable to send the enthusiastic signal desired by the bid's supporters. 'At that stage I didn't want to describe the level of ambivalence that existed within the Cabinet towards the bid,' Jowell explains. A week before the bid was due to be approved by Cabinet, the project looked to have hit a dead end.

Then on Wednesday, 15 January, came the first of two major breakthroughs. Jowell met Brown again and this time found him to be in a much more conciliatory mood. Her consensus-building was taking effect but the Chancellor was clear that there would be no Treasury money to pay for either the bid, which alone would cost £30 million, or the project itself if London won the vote.

'Gordon was absolutely clear,' says Jowell. 'He knew what the forecasts for the economy were and knew we would not be in a position to put huge amounts of government money into it.'

A day later Jowell called a meeting with the Mayor of London Ken Livingstone at her Cockspur Street office, over-looking Trafalgar Square. Jowell and Livingstone had known each other for over 25 years since their days together in London local government and there was mutual respect. As she waited for the Mayor to arrive, Jowell glanced at a picture on the wall of her office. It was a desolate scene depicting an isolated crossroads in the middle of the countryside, entitled *This is Nowhere*. She felt it was an appropriate image, for she too wondered where the Olympic vision was heading.

After months of delicate negotiations everything suddenly hinged on Livingstone, the maverick left winger. Relations between Tony Blair and Livingstone, better known in his earlier days as 'Red Ken', had broken down after a row over Livingstone's de-selection as a candidate in the London mayoral elections. Jowell knew that she couldn't allow him to steal the glory from the government should the Olympics get the green light. But she was also well aware that, without the financial backing of Livingstone, it was all over. 'You have to remember the level of suspicion about Ken within the government,' she recalls. 'But I had none of that. I had worked with him and known him for many years.

'He was not even in the Labour party at that point and there was suspicion of Ken. People questioned whether he could be trusted as a partner.' But Jowell banked on Livingstone's shared passion for the bid. And as they sat on white sofas, drinking tea and discussing Brown's ultimatum, it quickly became clear that the mayor was prepared to do whatever was needed to get the bid off the ground. Between 4 p.m. and 5 p.m. on the afternoon of Thursday, 16 January 2003, Livingstone and Jowell carved out a financial deal, which would cover the £2.4 billion public price tag of the Olympics if the bid was won.

The deal was a straightforward mix of cash from the national lottery and Londoners' money. One and a half billion pounds would come from the lottery – in particular a new Olympic scratch-card game – with the remaining £900 million from Livingstone through both the London Development Agency, his London regeneration body, and an increase in Londoners' council tax – the main local authority tax in the capital. Livingstone committed Londoners to a £20 a year increase in council tax for a maximum of 10 years. This deal might not have been welcomed by all Londoners faced with the prospect of higher taxes, but it went down very well in the Treasury, where Brown finally gave his outright blessing.

Livingstone's motivation for signing off the deal with Jowell was very different to hers. In a revealing admission he says his main priority was to obtain more money for investment in London. He recalls: 'For me at that stage I didn't think we had a cat in hell's chance of winning. But I was thinking this was a good chance to get some more money out of the government for Londoners. So I bid on that basis. It wasn't really until the Athens Games in August 2004 that I thought we could do it.

'Before the meeting with Tessa in January, there were stories in the papers saying that Gordon Brown said the bid would be dead unless the London council tax payers pay for it. I thought that had just been set up for me to say no and then I'd get blamed for killing the bid off. I did have my doubts that we could win it but I thought "let's go for it". When I went to the meeting with Tessa she was taken aback. She then sat down with my officials and we put together a credible deal. But we did come out of that meeting thinking, if we win the Games, it will have been a complete bloody accident.'

Regardless of Livingstone's motives, the deal was done and on Friday, 17 January, Jowell flew to Lausanne for a meeting with IOC President Rogge. Tony Blair needed to know whether the race for 2012 would be fair. He couldn't risk losing face to French President Jacques Chirac, especially at a time when Britain and France were in disagreement over the Iraq crisis and a range of European Union issues. Blair also wanted to avoid the embarrassing defeat suffered by England in the battle for the 2006 football World Cup – which went to Germany, while England's bid was condemned.

Jowell had to find out if Paris was a certainty to win. Rogge told her what she needed to hear. 'I told Jacques that I am driving the government towards this decision and need to know whether this is actually an open race or a competition that will lead to a Paris victory. He told me that 85 per cent of the bid is the candidate file and 15 per cent is geopolitical; whether the IOC members like you, whether they feel a sense of vision and passion for the Olympic movement. In a way I felt the technical side of it was easy and at that point I became convinced that we had to let the IOC know just how passionate we were.'

But she couldn't do that without first getting the approval of the government. Six days after she returned from Lausanne full of hope Blair gave his ministers another fortnight as he grappled with the growing problem of Iraq. This did, however, give officials more time to ensure the deal with Livingstone was watertight.

Once again, though, with the Cabinet set to give the go-ahead on February 13, the decision was put off. The Iraq crisis was now at the tipping point and Blair decided he could not be seen to be considering throwing a sports party just as he was about to ask British troops to fight for their country. 'The mood was moving in favour of bidding,' Jowell says. 'But our overriding preoccupation was Iraq, so he didn't really have time to focus on it.'

The first cruise missiles were not dropped on the Iraq capital Baghdad until 20 March and although the Saddam Hussein regime was toppled after just three weeks of fighting, there were continuing issues in Iraq. It was not until May that the Olympics were put back on the government's agenda. During that frustrating three-month delay, genuine fears began to surface among the bid's backers that the appetite for bringing the Games to London would be lost. Reedie says: 'The biggest downer at that time was not so much Tessa grappling with ministers, it was Iraq. It seemed that was such a diversion for the government. We understood the problem, but it was frustrating'.

According to Jowell the time delay allowed her Cabinet colleagues 'to really examine the figures and make a decision based on a fuller understanding of all the facts.'

With Saddam captured, the Cabinet agenda opened up and talks on the Games were rescheduled. Reedie remembers hearing the news that, at long last, the government was preparing to give its blessing. 'I was preparing to fly to Latvia for a meeting of the European Olympic Committee when I got a call from the Department of Culture, Media and Sport to go and see Tessa. She told me she thought it would go through. I asked her what we would do if it didn't, because if it hadn't gone through the next day then it would have had to wait another few weeks because of the Whitsun recess. I said to Tessa that if it got put off again that would be it. We simply wouldn't have time to do this and so we would pull the plug. It sounds pretty dramatic now but it really was that touch and go.'

When the 15 May meeting arrived Jowell was nervous. She even bought a new suit for her presentation. Ahead of the meeting, she met Blair to make sure she had his support and they agreed that if the government said no to the bid then they would have to answer the very difficult question as to why London, the capital of the country and the fourth largest economy in the world, was not even prepared to try. At the meeting the Cabinet was unanimous in its backing, Jowell recalls, 'It was a fabulous feeling. After grappling with so many projects that had gone wrong I had always believed passionately that the Olympics could be and would be different. I had bought into the vision of how London could be transformed by the Games and I was determined not to let it go.'

As for Blair himself, he acknowledges the role Jowell played in persuading the Cabinet to back London. He says: 'Tessa was a very important influence. She was absolutely certain that we had to go for it. And Cherie, too, played a big part. But they were pushing at an open door to a great extent. I thought, if we could pull it off. it would be a fantastic thing for this country.

'I am not going to pretend that there wasn't real debate in government. There was. But, in the end, we all decided that we should go for it and John Prescott was critical in swinging everyone behind the decision.'

Craig Reedie recalls: 'Tessa did a magnificent job and deserves great credit for getting it through the Cabinet. But she learned that Olympic bids cannot be led by politicians and governments who by their very nature have to compromise and debate. If they had led the bid from that moment on, we would have found it difficult to build momentum.'

From his office in Nyon, on the outskirts of Geneva, Mike Lee watched these events unfolding with an increasingly keen interest. In late 2002, as the government began to wrestle with the decision of whether to bid or not, Lee was enjoying life as the director of communications and public affairs with European football's ruling body UEFA. The cut and thrust of Westminster could not have been more removed from the tranquil surroundings of UEFA's stylish glass and chrome headquarters on the banks of Lake Geneva.

Lee had spent much of his working life among the spin doctors and those involved in policy in the creation and development of New Labour. A former adviser to MP David Blunkett in the late 80s and early 90s during Blunkett's days as shadow minister on local government and then health, Lee joined UEFA in 2000 after a successful six-year spell working for consultancy company Westminster Strategy, where his work included acting as press chief for English football's Premier League. His UEFA brief was wide, and included heading up the organisation's communications team.

For the next two years, he was constantly on the road: one day Madrid for a Champions League game, the next Kiev for a key meeting of UEFA executives.

It was a thrilling and important job and although it meant spending a long time apart from his wife Heather, his then 10-year-old son Alex and 20-year-old stepson Euan, it was an exciting time. Lee recalls: 'Taking the UEFA job was a big decision but the right one. It was a great challenge but I could only see my family at weekends and on holidays. I was often away on the road with UEFA and that meant there wasn't too much time to myself, but there were times when I missed them a lot.'

Eager not to be away from home for too long, Lee had always planned to review his time working in Switzerland after three years. So when news began to filter through to him that there was a serious possibility of a London bid, his antennae started to flicker. 'I had tuned into it quite early on through government and sports contacts,' Lee explains. 'I found the prospect of a London bid fascinating. At the same time, I knew the political scene well enough back in London to know that there were difficulties. The war in Iraq also meant that it was not a top priority. My sense of it was that it was a potentially interesting project but that there were clearly some huge obstacles to overcome.

'It was also clear that Tessa had worked very hard to get it through. She convinced the Prime Minister early on but she had to convince the rest of the Cabinet. I had already been sounded out by contacts from the bid that they might be looking for a communications director, so when it was eventually signed off in May I started to let it be known that I was very interested. I spoke at length to Richard Caborn, who was very helpful in backing my appointment.'

Lee felt that he had the right mix of political understanding and sporting knowledge to help keep London's bid on track. He understood that Britain's voracious media would make a two-year campaign even more difficult. There would be no patriotic tub thumping from Fleet Street. But he was convinced he had the credentials in the demanding worlds of communications and public affairs. 'What I was bringing to the party, hopefully, was this combination of a good understanding of the British and international media, particularly the sports media, and interesting experience of front-line politics and political campaigning. I also knew the key political figures involved. Tessa Jowell and Richard Caborn I knew very well and I had a way into Tony Blair and people inside Number 10 Downing Street. In a way, when I looked at what was needed to devise a communications strategy and deal with the complexities of the political world, I felt that I had something to offer London.'

Lee was born the son of a miner in the north-east mining village of Boldon Colliery in South Tyneside. His father Richard lost one of his legs in a mining accident and was forced to retire early. His mother had always helped support the family by working in the community as a home help. Times were tough but Lee studied hard and won a place at the Royal Grammar School in Newcastle upon Tyne. He went on to secure a place at St Peter's College, Oxford where he read politics, philosophy and economics.

'I come from pretty humble origins,' Lee said. 'It's been a pretty interesting journey for me from a coal-mining town to an Oxford graduate.

'People don't always realise my background when I speak to them. Once, long before we were married, I was having a row with my first wife Helen about the class system. We were both working for David Blunkett at the time and were keen to make our mark politically. She was arguing that I had no idea about what it was like to be working class and joked that the next thing I would tell her was that my father was a one-legged miner. Well, the look on my face said it all as I slowly explained to her that in fact my father was indeed a one-legged miner. No one likes that story more than my dad!'

After university, Lee moved to Leicester and became a teacher and local councillor. He was a devoted left-winger but a move to London in the mid-1980s and his work for Labour frontbencher Blunkett put him on the road to becoming a supporter of Tony Blair's New Labour project. While he carved out a place for himself in the political scene at Westminster, however, one other passion burned fiercely in him. Sport and, in particular, Sunderland FC.

'Football was always number one in our house and Sunderland was my first love. I started watching them back in 1963/64. That was a legendary team led by the great defender Charlie Hurley and we were promoted from the old second division. Average gates at Roker Park in those days were big – over forty thousand – and for a six-year-old boy it was a thrilling experience.

'One of the greatest moments for me was watching "the lads" win the 1973 FA Cup final when Sunderland beat Leeds United 1-0. Moments like that mean that football will always be a passion for me.'

As a youngster, Lee was a respectable sportsman himself too. At his primary school, Hedworth Lane Junior in Boldon Colliery, he was to become captain of the school football and cricket teams. To win entry to the highly regarded Royal Grammar School from such a small mining town like Boldon was unprecedented. However, it left Lee with mixed feelings as the school was fiercely traditional and didn't play football. Rugby was the sport of choice. It was a tough decision, but he took up the new game with relish, honing his skills as a flanker before going on to captain the school's first XV. He was also

awarded the honour of representing the county of Northum-
berland in rugby at schoolboy level.

His speed in those days was his greatest asset and he was
also an accomplished runner. He enjoyed athletics and ran the
200 and 100 metres for his county and his school. He also
played cricket for the school's first team.

At university, however, politics took over and his own
sporting career took a back seat. He became an active socialist
with strong views and suddenly playing rugby didn't fit with
his politics. 'In those days it felt like it was the sport of the
Establishment,' he explains. But his enthusiasm for athletics
and the Olympic Games never wavered. 'I always loved the
Olympics. Like Seb Coe, my first memory of the Games was
watching the 1968 Olympics on TV from Mexico City. I was
eleven at the time and I remember watching, thrilled, as David
Hemery won gold. It was clear to me from a very early age that
the Olympics were very special and as I grew older I kept a
close eye on most Olympic sports. Where I grew up there was
a strong interest in athletics and especially those sons of the
north-east like Brendan Foster and Steve Cram. But I was also
fascinated by the Coe versus Ovett battles. And I have to admit
that in those days I was slightly more with Ovett than Coe.'

With sport such a major part of his professional life, Lee's
main contact with the grass roots of sport these days comes
through watching his son Alex play rugby and football for his
school. 'As well as being an immensely proud father, the
mornings standing on the touchline actually bring home the
reality of how important a part sport plays in so many people's
lives. A love of sport, and all that it represents, starts early in
life and therefore getting young people involved is a real
challenge. I never lost sight of that throughout the bid.'

It's this broad range of experiences that made Lee a vital
target for the London Olympic bid team. His ability to handle
the cut and thrust of the political jungle and his understanding
of what makes sport tick meant he was perhaps uniquely
qualified for the job of handling the way the media during
London's campaign. It was never likely to be an easy job –
there was much cynicism among the British press towards the
country's past efforts to land major sporting events. The

campaign needed someone who could help turn that image around and also plug the damaging leaks which emanated from the many different groups involved in the prospective London bid.

Lee has a formidable reputation among the British sports press. He is known as the 'spinmeister', one of the first communications executives to merge the world of politics and sport. At a time when New Labour spin doctors like Alistair Campbell were becoming big news for their ruthless methods, Lee became known, initially through his work for the Premier League, as a man who understood the press's needs but who would not bend easily to them.

Inside sport he had became recognised as a loyal and trusted operator who was prepared to get his hands dirty and work tirelessly to promote and defend those he represented.

The London Olympic bid was perfect for him and with the campaign swinging into action, he was sure he did not want to miss out.

2. TAKING OFF

The first thing that struck Mike Lee as he walked through the doors of London 2012's new headquarters on the fiftieth floor of Canary Wharf on the Isle of Dogs was the view. He had grown used to the picturesque setting of his UEFA offices beside Lake Geneva, but this was something else. London stretched out for miles all around him. To the west the Thames glistened in the sunlight as it wound its way through the capital, past the congested office blocks of the City, past the majestic dome of St Paul's and on towards Westminster. To the north, the run-down wasteland of the Lee Valley, a forgotten dumping ground which would be transformed if London won the 2012 Games. Behind and to the south sat the Dome, a constant reminder of the challenge of grand projects. Lee felt exhilarated.

The second thing he noticed as Barbara Cassani, the glamorous American chosen to lead the bid, strode towards him, wearing a power suit and smiling warmly from ear to ear, was how empty the office was. There were hardly any desks or computers and only a handful of chairs. Suddenly the enormity of what he was about to take on dawned on him.

'You literally had to grab any chair you could find in order to hold a meeting,' says Lee. 'I knew that it was early days for the bid but I didn't realise that it was essentially starting from scratch. They had just moved into the offices at Canary Wharf.

When people talk about the bid having to make a standing start that is a massive understatement. I just felt we had so much to do in just two years and, yes, I admit it, I was daunted.'

Although Lee had not yet agreed to accept Cassani's offer to become the communications and public affairs director of London's bid, he was becoming increasingly excited about the prospect of playing a leading role in the project. At the time of their meeting in the autumn of 2003, Cassani had only been in the job of chairman of London 2012 for a month or so herself, having officially started work on 1 August. Given the size of the task ahead she was determined not to waste any time.

Lee and Cassani had met twice before. With each meeting Lee was becoming more drawn in by Cassani's enthusiasm.

He explains: 'One of the reasons I became convinced to do it was Barbara. She was very eloquent about the bid. She used the phrase to me that "the stars are aligned for London". Her energy, drive and determination were so infectious. That was a big factor behind my decision to accept the offer.'

Lee told Cassani of his decision a couple of weeks after that trip to Canary Wharf. 'I was in the Czech Republic for a very busy UEFA executive meeting,' he recalls. 'I had made my decision. It was a good time for me to come back home, so I rang Barbara from Prague to tell her I had accepted the job. She was a little bit surprised, I think, but seemed delighted.'

But Lee wasn't relying on instinct alone as he signed on the dotted line for London 2012. He had also used his wide network of contacts in the international media and Westminster to gauge how good London's chances were of beating its rivals and securing the Games. He even went to see Christophe de Kepper, the influential adviser to IOC President Jacques Rogge, to ask him about London's chances. 'I had to know whether we had a realistic chance,' he said. 'Being involved in an Olympic bid was going to be very special and London was a good candidate and could be a serious contender. But at that point the consensus was that Paris would win easily. I was going to give up a very nice job in UEFA, where I was about to be offered a new contract which would have meant another four years' commitment. It was a big decision to make and I needed to know the truth.

'The message that came back was that London had problems and issues to address but that two years was a good time to develop a campaign and London had something to offer. I was told London could not be ruled out. That was good enough for me.'

While Lee had been persuaded to take a gamble based on informal soundings from senior IOC insiders and Cassani's raw passion for the project, not everyone shared Lee's initial admiration for Cassani. When the 42-year-old Boston-born businesswoman was appointed on 16 June, commentators were split. Her supporters pointed to her energy and determination. She had set up British Airways' budget airline Go from nothing in 1998 with just £25 million. By the time it was sold in a management buy-out four years later its value had soared to £374 million and it had full-year profits of £4.2 million. Cassani benefited significantly and picked up the 2002 Businesswoman of the Year award for good measure.

Now she was charged with another start-up company, this time an Olympic bid. She insisted she was perfectly qualified for such an overwhelming task. 'I built a company from scratch in just six months,' she told reporters at a press conference to announce her appointment as bid chairman. 'I remember my first day at Go, when I had a mobile phone and nothing else.'

But, her critics replied, an Olympic bid was very different to running an airline. The International Olympic Committee is a unique organisation consisting of around 120 members drawn from royal families, business life and the world of sport. These mainly middle-aged men like nothing more than cutting political deals in return for their precious vote. It was not a world she was used to or, her critics claimed, one to which she seemed much inclined to become accustomed.

The fact she was an American created a major headache for London's bid team. Some IOC members said it would cause confusion at a time when New York was also bidding for the 2012 Olympics. There was also strong anti-American sentiment within the IOC caused by the fall-out from the troubled organisation of the 1996 Atlanta Games and the corruption scandal in 1999 that arose from the Salt Lake City bid victory. There was also a danger that IOC members would not understand why Britain could not find a Briton to front London's bid.

The bid team defended the decision to appoint Cassani, saying nationality was not an issue and that it in fact demonstrated the cosmopolitan make-up of London. They added that she was the latest in a series of inspirational women to front a city's Olympic bid: Gianna Angelopoulos-Daskalaki won the 1997 vote for Athens to host the 2004 Olympics (she later returned to ensure the Athens Games opened on time); while the Italian businesswoman Evelina Christillin fronted Turin's successful bid for the 2006 Winter Olympics.

The Sports Minister Richard Caborn likened opposition to Cassani's appointment to the same jingoistic criticisms that accompanied Swede Sven-Goran Eriksson's rise to become the England football manager. 'The nationality of the chairman is not an issue,' Caborn told the *Daily Mail*. 'London is the most cosmopolitan of places and foreign leaders are now accepted in every area of sport.'

However, whatever the case about her nationality, the truth about Cassani is that she was never the first choice for the post of chairman of the bid. She had been identified by City headhunting firm Saxton Bampfylde Hever as a chief executive who could be charged with the task of getting the project off the ground and delivering the technical part of the bid. She was perfect for that job, as her time at Go had proved.

The aim was to find a British-born chairman to work alongside her. One by one, however, the big hitters of industry and politics withdrew from the race. Sir Christopher Meyer, the former British ambassador to Washington during the Bill Clinton administration, was the candidate most favoured by the British Olympic Association. He had a close understanding of the inner workings of Number 10 Downing Street, even though his memoirs, published much later, would expose a deep rift between Meyer, Tony Blair and senior figures at the very top of the Labour government, particularly over the Iraq war. Meyer and his wife Catherine were seen as the archetypal networkers, ideal for the round of Olympic meetings and sports events where they would be called upon to meet and greet important people and push London's case. Between them they spoke nine different languages and could draw on all their years of diplomatic parties and contacts to support Britain's campaign.

But Meyer had also recently taken a job as head of the Press Complaints Commission. In the end he felt he had too much to do to take on another major role. On 5 June 2003 he let ministers know that, while he was deeply flattered, he did not wish his name to go forward for the shortlist.

That list was getting shorter by the day. Charles Allen, then chairman of Granada Television, was too busy pushing through the crucial merger with Carlton to form a single ITV company. Sir Christopher Gent, the former Vodafone chief executive; Sir Christopher Bland, the former chairman of the BBC who later moved to run British Telecom; Gerry Robinson, chairman of the Arts Council; and Lord Simon of Highbury, former chairman of BP, were all linked with the job. They all let it be known that, after much deliberation, they did not want it.

The headhunters spoke to ITN newsreader Trevor McDonald and also consulted the Prime Minister's wife Cherie Blair as the net widened. But the one name that kept coming back was that of Barbara Cassani. Mayor of London Ken Livingstone was convinced she was the right person to lead the bid. Livingstone had a track record for hiring successful Americans for key British jobs, having lured Bob Kiley from his position running New York's subway network to London as the transport commissioner.

In the end, as all the other leading candidates fell by the wayside, it came down to a straight choice between Cassani and Kevin Roberts, the New Zealand-born worldwide chief executive of advertising giants Saatchi & Saatchi. Cassani won.

BOA chairman and IOC member, Craig Reedie, was part of the selection panel that developed the final shortlist. He recalls favouring Sir Christopher Meyer but backing Cassani once it became clear that she was the choice of both the government and Mayor Livingstone. 'Barbara's huge advantage was that she could start tomorrow. If I had said no we would have had to start the headhunting process again and we would never have got to the starting line.

'She came in with bags of energy and a few of her friends and made a start. She knew nothing about the Olympic world. But slowly she built it up and got us under way.'

Livingstone never had any such doubts. 'She was the outstanding candidate to do the job,' he says. 'You had a year to go from zero to have a total bid and you needed someone full time, who could start immediately and a manic person who drives everyone forward and she stood out as the only person who was going to do that. If we hadn't appointed her we would not have had a credible bid by the end of the year. Only she could have created a plan that was credible and only she had the drive to do it.'

Mike Lee admired Cassani for the way she allowed him a free hand in setting up his own team. He says: 'One of the great things about Barbara was she gave me permission to recruit the people I wanted to bring in within the structure and numbers we agreed. It was important that she understood that my role would be both communications and public affairs. That freed me up to make a number of key appointments. Jackie Brock-Doyle had been acting as a consultant to the bid team and, although there had been public relations problems, she had been one of the key players in the early days and she came with experience of working in bids and major events. From her I also learned about Michael Pirrie who had great contacts, especially in the world of the Olympic media where I was perhaps not as well connected at that stage. John Zerafa was someone I had worked with before in consultancy and I chose him to work closely on building political relations. They were undoubtedly my three key appointments in setting up the team.'

At the same time as he was bringing in his own staff, Lee also took two other crucial PR decisions which made a massive difference to the bid. The first was to remove PR specialists Brunswick Group from the campaign. Brunswick enjoyed close links to Cassani but specialise in financial PR and were newcomers in the sports world. 'I saw very quickly the limitations of the PR agency,' said Lee. 'They were excellent in the City but in my view had limited experience of the cut and thrust of the sports media. I saw early on that we needed to build an in-house team with real experts and people focused on the bid. We had to understand the need for discipline, including an end to leaks, and the development of a genuine bid script. The building of an in-house PR team was a priority.'

The other potential hindrance to the London team building a good relationship with much of the media was the bid's close links with the *Daily Telegraph*. The paper had staged an impressive campaign to pressure the government into bidding but many rival publications felt the links between the bid and the *Telegraph* were too close. Lee decided to address the problem: 'The bid had great relations with the sports section of the *Daily Telegraph* which was fine but it had clearly led to some hostility from all the other daily newspapers. There was a need to develop those relationships through sports editors and key journalists without losing the *Telegraph*. This did lead to difficulties at the time but the rest of Fleet Street could see that I was serious about it. We met key people from the other newspapers to emphasise our changing approach and ensured that stories and features were more widely spread.'

Despite such positive early steps, there were storm clouds brewing over Cassani's appointment. From the very beginning the omens were not good. Cassani and Brunswick had planned to unveil the American as bid leader on the south bank of the Thames opposite a magnificent backdrop of St Paul's Cathedral and the City. But there was embarrassment all round as children from a residents' group in nearby Coin Street, Waterloo hijacked the press conference. They were angry that a grant for £450,000 promised to develop playing fields had not materialised. Every time Cassani attempted to do an interview or pose for a picture, the kids would start chanting anti-Olympic slogans and waving banners. Having taken refuge on a tiny restaurant balcony in the nearby Oxo Tower, she then had to fend off negative questions about her nationality and experience for the demanding role. Although she gave a slick performance, the press conference had been a mess and only served to confirm many people's fears about London's hopes of winning the two-year battle with favourites Paris.

Cassani kept her head down after that. She did few public appearances and instead started work on building the team of executives that could help her convince her critics. She poached a handful of key players from Go, the most notable of which was David Magliano, who became marketing director. He would play a crucial role in helping formulate the London Olympic vision that would prove so crucial.

She also made Granada Chief Charles Allen, one of the top candidates for the post of chairman, vice chairman, as she also did with former Olympic hurdler turned athletics promoter Alan Pascoe. Slowly the team was building and the offices at Canary Wharf, just an empty shell a couple of months earlier, were beginning to fill up.

Cassani's first opportunity to experience the Olympic family came at the start of July as the IOC Session met in the Czech capital Prague to choose the host city for the 2010 Winter Olympics. Although the Winter Games might appear to have little to do with the election of the summer hosts due two years later, there were crucial lessons to be learned and important people for Cassani and her team to meet.

In addition, victory for the Canadian favourite Vancouver would undermine New York's bid for the 2012 Summer Games. IOC watchers predicted the members would not back successive Olympics in North America. In the end the Canadians won but only by the slimmest of margins. Just three votes separated them from the unlikely South Korean city of Pyeongchang. It was a revealing lesson in how close the contests could become and the importance of effective lobbying and slick presentations in front of the IOC.

Cassani did not impress Olympic observers the following month when she failed to turn up for the start of the World Athletics Championships in Paris. Given the backdrop of the Picketts Lock fiasco, London knew it had a lot of ground to make up with the senior figures in charge of track and field and yet Cassani only arrived in the French capital in the second week of the Championships, when most IOC members had left. She defended herself telling the London *Evening Standard*:

'The most important thing at the moment is to work on the technical bid. I believe only once you have the technical bid together can you then go into the earnest process of lobbying. I felt it was more important for me to be at home interviewing candidates for senior positions. I take a long-term view on the lobbying. If the nuts and bolts work that's the priority. It's about personal style.'

At the same time, however, stories began to surface that Cassani would be sacked long before the final IOC decision in July 2005. One report, carried by the news agency Agence France Presse (AFP) and written by the respected Olympics reporter Erskine McCulloch, claimed London's bid was beset by internal splits and that Cassani was under pressure from government ministers over her style of management. 'I do not expect her to be in charge when the vote is taken,' a government source was quoted as saying in the AFP report. It turned out to be a very prescient comment.

Perhaps it was in response to the growing doubts or perhaps it was great vision on her part but, in September 2003, Cassani made what turned out to be her most important appointment. Sebastian Coe was made a vice-chairman of the bid (bringing the number to three) and handed the job of fostering good relationships and lobbying the IOC. Hiring the double Olympic champion, who had won the 1500m in Los Angeles and Moscow, was seen as a shrewd move by Cassani.

Coe was still viewed with great fondness within the IOC, especially by the former President Juan Antonio Samaranch, who at one stage began grooming Coe to become a future IOC President. Coe was on the council of the International Association of Athletics Federations (IAAF) and was therefore coming into regular contact with the people who would make the key decision on the 2012 Games. He was also politically experienced, having been a Conservative MP and special adviser and Private Secretary to former Tory leader William Hague.

And yet, interestingly and, with hindsight, surprisingly, his promotion to a key role on the bid was met with some raised eyebrows by people within the British sporting establishment.

Some people in athletics regarded Coe as an unfulfilled talent in the world of sports administration.

Hiring Coe showed Cassani had learned some harsh lessons. She now knew the bid was hugely different to setting up an airline. She admitted: 'The IOC sees its role as being quasi-diplomatic in many ways. When you think about the Olympics in that light, it raises it above the political agenda. It's something that's sacred to people. I approached it like a business person at the beginning and I had to stand back from it a little bit and think: Whoa, it's important that we treasure bringing the Games here. This is not about business.

'We are using public money, so there's a whole load of obligations that go with that. I may be spearheading an Olympic bid but there are lots of organisations who have to deliver, and if they don't play their role, we can't win the Games. So this is different from managing a business. It's more like managing a campaign. I need to get out there and meet people.'

At the same time as the penny was finally dropping with Cassani, so Mike Lee was preparing to make the switch from Switzerland to join her team. For the last three months of 2003 he split his time between his old and new roles. It was a demanding period, but he was still involved in some key issues within football, including brokering talks between the English and Turkish Football Associations designed to ensure there would be no trouble between rival fans when the two teams met in a critical European Championship qualifier that October.

This transition gave Lee some time to explore the way the bid's message was being sold to the media. He didn't like what he saw and was keen to get started to make changes he believed were vital if London was to make up the ground it had lost early on.

His concerns were perfectly illustrated by the way his very own appointment was leaked a day before the official announcement. Having finally found a chief executive in Keith Mills, a millionaire sailing fanatic who had founded the hugely successful Air Miles and Nectar loyalty card schemes, the bid team planned to announce his appointment on Friday, 26

September. Mills was himself then supposed to reveal Mike Lee's appointment in a hand-picked briefing for Sunday newspaper journalists. Mills's name appeared in the papers on the Friday morning while Lee's was leaked to the Saturday papers. Lee knew at that point that he would have to find a way of plugging the leaks – and fast.

Lee was also becoming increasingly aware of how important the communications strategy would be to the eventual outcome of the race for 2012. For the first time, media strategy and vision would be more important than shady deals carved out in hotel corridors – for this was to be a bidding contest unlike any other. The Olympic movement had set down tough new rules for bidding cities following the Salt Lake City corruption scandal. Although corruption within the Olympic movement had been suspected for decades, this 1999 episode finally exposed the dark underbelly of the Olympic family – a world where cash was expected in return for votes, a world where five-star hotels, lavish hospitality and luxury gifts were readily available.

When Salt Lake City won the right to host the Winter Games in 2002, Tom Welch, the bid leader, and Dave Johnson, his deputy, took the credit. But just two years after the Utah state capital won the vote in 1995, Welch resigned. He was replaced by a former mine boss Frank Joklik, who had an entirely different way of dealing with people. The result was a leaked memo from one disaffected committee member to a local TV news station outlining details of how Salt Lake organisers were paying for scholarships for the sons and daughters of some IOC members.

At first, the response to the story was slow but eventually the information found its way to the Swiss IOC member Marc Hodler, a lawyer, who used the evidence to start putting pressure on his colleagues. It was soon discovered that six members were receiving 'humanitarian aid' through the scholarship programme. Hodler claimed some Olympic 'agents' had been involved in vote-buying for a decade and he believed there were IOC members who could be bought.

In response to the scandal, the then IOC President Juan Antonio Samaranch pushed through a series of reforms at the end of 1999, including a blanket ban on visits by IOC members to bidding cities. In future only the evaluation commission, made up of experts and powerful IOC members would be allowed to visit cities and then report back to the members with a detailed report on each bid. The evaluation commission team would make one visit to each city and inspect their facilities and plans and meet with key government figures.

At the same time all gifts unless of a nominal value were banned and bidding cities were given strict rules on when they could visit IOC events to lobby. An IOC ethics commission was set up to enforce the rules and keep a close eye on rival cities to ensure they were focusing on their bids and not attacking each other's. When Jacques Rogge took over as IOC President in July 2001 he vowed to keep the strict regulations in place. The rules were extremely tight and inevitably cities began to look at how they could campaign effectively without directly breaking the rules.

Mike Lee knew that in the post-Salt Lake City world of the IOC, there had to be other ways of gaining an advantage over London's rivals. In 2003, these rivals were eight other world famous cities: Cuban capital Havana, Leipzig in eastern Germany, Rio de Janeiro in Brazil, Istanbul in Turkey, New York, Moscow, Paris and Madrid. President Rogge promised to cut at least three from the battle early on to allow a more manageable competition but the early days of bidding were a frenzied experience and the IOC became even more watchful.

Lee says: 'One of the most important things to understand about the 2012 campaign was that this was the first Summer Olympic campaign to be held under a completely new set of rules put in place following the Salt Lake scandal. A lot of the traditional things that had been accepted in previous bids such as visits to cities and gifts were completely outlawed.

'We needed to break new ground in terms of developing a modern campaign, which needed to have communications and marketing at its heart because there was the real possibility that direct contact with the members would be very limited. The technical side of the bid was always going to be important but it was the selling of the bid and what it could mean for the Olympic movement which was at the heart of the challenge.'

With that in mind he and his team started devising the framework of a campaign that would become the template for all modern Olympic bids.

Lee breaks it down into a number of key elements. He says: 'We were very conscious early on of the need to maintain momentum over a two-year period. We thought about the campaign in distinct phases, developing the messages and a range of events to ensure there was pace and energy. There were milestones to build our communications around but we also needed other hooks and storylines to keep the pace high.

'It was essentially like an international political campaign. We needed to understand our audiences and develop a global election manifesto. Building domestic support was important but it was just one part of the game. At times this made us unpopular with the wider group of stakeholders who felt we should have been paying closer attention to their demands. But we were clearly focused on the objective and that was to win in Singapore. We had to hold our nerve at times and we never lost sight of the main goal which was to gain support internationally.

'We also set about developing key themes that we could reinforce through presentations and communications events. The core elements were regeneration of the East End of London, the diversity of London, the legacy of the Games, use of London's landmark iconic sites and what the Olympics could offer British and world sport. Early on we also began to develop an idea of Games for the next generation.

'We also varied our themes, depending on our audience. We think that in this area we definitely gained an advantage over our rivals. We worked hard on our core messages and began planning how to deploy them over the campaign. We were developing the ingredients for what was to become London's story.

'Finally, and this was just as vital to our success, we had to get the best use of the star personalities connected to the bid. We had some great names in Sebastian Coe, five-times gold-medal-winning rower, Steve Redgrave, double Olympic champions, Kelly Holmes and Daley Thompson, Olympic heptathlon champion, Denise Lewis, four-times gold-medal-winning rower, Matthew Pinsent and the great British paralympian Tanni Grey-Thompson. These were icons of the Olympic movement. We wanted the IOC to know we were using athletes to devise our plans and had athletes directly involved in the bid. This became an important part of the PR mix. The stars stimulated interest in London's bid and helped build up a feeling that this bid was about sport and took sport seriously. They were not just there for photo opportunities but each sporting ambassador symbolised a key element of the bid – they were part of the narrative.

'There's a lot of interest around the world in how London did it because it was a whole new style of campaigning. There was a commitment to evolving the campaign because the way the ground rules shifted meant we had to be nimble and dynamic. Over the course of the campaign London set the pace and I think the others found that quite difficult.

'We spent a lot of time internally talking about how we could develop the overall narrative of the bid. We didn't want just unconnected themes or events – we were striving to tell London's story to the Olympic movement and that distinguished us from other cities in the race. We knew we could be distinctive, but the big question we didn't know the answer to in the early days was whether it would finally appeal to the IOC members. For us that was always the question we came back to – how can we develop a campaign that will attract votes and give us a chance of winning.'

As the bid began to find its feet in the dawn of 2004, it had already been an incredible journey. And yet, through all the doubts, and from the government hesitation to the early criticism of Cassani, Lee was convinced London had a story to tell. He just couldn't be sure at this stage whether it had a fairy-tale ending.

3. A DAY AT THE OPERA

M ike Lee looked on nervously from the wings of the Royal Opera House. This great setting, he thought to himself, had played host to some of the world's finest singers and musicians. It was impossible not to be overawed as he reflected on the greats of opera who had performed in this iconic venue.

But now, as his boss Barbara Cassani rose to speak, all those names faded into irrelevance. Suddenly the only thing that mattered to the London team in the first month of 2004 was her speech. Lee knew she could not afford to make a mistake.

Cassani, along with PM Tony Blair and London Mayor Ken Livingstone were showcasing London's bid for the first time. The Opera House launch was a major moment for the capital's campaign and it was essential that all the key players hit the right notes. Despite all the first night nerves, Cassani, Blair and Livingstone pulled it off.

London's launch had gone without a hitch and, at last, after months of waiting, the bid was officially under way. Lee recalls: 'The launch was a significant milestone for us. You have to remember that, up until that stage, we were still facing a lot of media criticism. This really allowed us to start banging the drum for London.'

Although London had declared its bid way back in May 2003 and had been building its plans slowly from its head-quarters on the fiftieth floor of Canary Wharf, the campaign had kept a relatively low profile. Now, in the early weeks of January 2004, the time had come to start moving through the PR gears with the official launch.

Lee and London's bid leaders knew that their rivals would be planning similar launches to coincide with the first official milestone on the road to the International Olympic Committee vote in Singapore on 6 July 2005.

On 15 January the IOC required all the cities to submit an applicant questionnaire outlining the basic details of their bids. All nine cities; London, Paris, Madrid, New York, Moscow, Leipzig, Havana, Rio de Janeiro and Istanbul were asked to answer thirty questions on wide-ranging issues such as government support, finance, transport and venue plans. It was a long way from the 600-page report that would have to be filed with the IOC that November for those who made it on to the IOC final shortlist. Nevertheless it needed a lot of work.

Since assuming her role as chairman of the bid in August 2003, Cassani had focused intently on the task of getting the technical part of the bid right. That meant assessing venues, outlining a new Olympic Park and appointing the right team to spearhead the bid. This played to her strength for kick-starting a new enterprise. The actual job of selling London's bid to the British public, the rest of the world and, most importantly, the voting IOC members, was still a secondary consideration. What was the point of making a big noise until you had a story to tell? she argued.

The London team knew that the French were planning a major bash on the first floor of the Eiffel Tower and that the Spanish Prime Minister was planning an extravagant show to be staged in his own Madrid palace. Lee and bid marketing director David Magliano were determined that London would upstage them and grab the world's attention. They began work in the later months of 2003 on securing a knockout venue and a top-class cast list to help the Brits steal the limelight.

Lee recalls: 'We all were aware that the applicant questionnaire had to be filed with the IOC on 15 January. We only had to answer thirty questions so it was just the bare bones of the bid but it was the foundation stone for the future and could be used to really mark the first phase of the public campaign.

There had already been a lot of discussion internally about the choice of sport venues, the creation of legacy, the potential shape of the Olympic Park. But the key at this point was to answer the IOC's questions.

'So one of the challenges was to find a way of making it exciting without having a great amount of substance to promote.

'At this stage no one else had done their formal launch but we were aware that the other cities had published details of their plans. They were more advanced than we were and had been up and running for much longer. Everyone kept telling me that Paris was so far down the track as to be unbeatable but we held our nerve. There was still more than eighteen months to go. Barbara had set in motion a lot of detailed work and we were confident that once we launched we could truly get the race going.

'At that point I was still very much fresh in the job, but I was sure it presented a fantastic opportunity to get on the front foot almost for the first time. Up until this point there had been no detail of London's plans made public.

'There had been a lot of criticism about the lack of government support so I knew that if we were going to make an impact with our launch then we had to get the Prime Minister there. I started talks with Number 10 in late December and got a response in early January confirming that he would definitely be there. The political line-up would include Mayor Ken Livingstone and the Culture Secretary Tessa Jowell.

'We decided to be quite ambitious and for the first time the partnership with David Magliano started to feel good. We decided on the Royal Opera House because it was such an iconic venue and offered such great flexibility. We could use one of the theatres for the formal launch and then we could use the Floral Hall to put on a series of sporting exhibitions by kids from the East End. It was perfect.'

This was the first chance Lee and his team had to tell people how a London Games would be organised.

The show was produced by events company Live, which specialises in this kind of occasion, and Lee secured support from the BBC and Sue Barker, the face of the corporation's Olympic coverage, agreed to present it. The plan was to base the thirty-minute presentation around a video, profiling London's plans, and speeches by Blair, Cassani, Livingstone and Jowell. Although it had been well trailed for months that the London bid would be centred around a new Olympic Park and stadium to be built on wasteland at Stratford, the whole vision for the capital had not been aired so publicly before.

Then there were to be a series of interviews with the stars in the audience. Sir Steve Redgrave and Lord Sebastian Coe spoke with Sue Barker to tell the world why London would be the Games for the athletes. At that stage Coe could not have possibly seen how far-sighted the words he uttered that day would become: 'We would not be doing this unless we were convinced London can win,' he told the audience. 'London can stage a brilliant Olympic Games.'

Messages of support were also delivered from present-day athletes including Britain's marathon world-record-holder Paula Radcliffe and Matthew Pinsent, who at that stage was a member of the IOC, and World and Olympic triple jump champion Jonathan Edwards.

The launch was designed to be as slick as the BBC's showpiece annual event, Sports Personality of the Year, and it certainly had the same highly professional feel. 'We had a lot of help from the BBC and presenter Sue Barker made it work very, very well,' said Lee. 'She was a true professional and made it flow. It was much more than a PR event. It was a genuine launch.

'We also paid attention to diversity and so we had a good mix of Olympic athletes, Paralympic athletes and people from different communities and cultures. This was a chance to start getting the messages across that would carry all the way through to Singapore: legacy, diversity, regeneration, government support and passion for sport. These were to become our key themes and they hadn't really been aired before so forcefully.'

Lee and Magliano also wanted to use the launch as a way to practise the bid team's presentational skills. Though it wasn't for eighteen months, they already sensed the final presentation to the IOC in Singapore would be crucial. They wanted to extol strict professionalism and slick production.

But they never lost sight of the principal point of the launch and that was to explain, for the first time in as much detail as was agreed at that stage, how and where a London Games would be staged – a mix of the new and the old of the capital. The opening and closing ceremonies, and the athletics, would take place in a new 80,000-seater stadium to be built at Stratford in East London – a new cathedral for British sport. Nearby would be the Olympic village for 15,000 athletes, coaches and officials. In total 17 of the 28 sports on the Olympic programme would be staged at the new Olympic Park, to be built on Lee Valley wasteland. A new velodrome, aquatics complex and hockey stadium would be included as part of the state of the art facilities.

The rest of the sports would be staged at a mix of landmark locations and traditional London sporting arenas. Tennis, for example, would take place at Wimbledon, home of the All England Lawn Tennis Club. The football finals would be at the new Wembley Stadium and archery would be held at Lord's – home of English cricket. Rowing would take place on a refurbished complex at Eton School's Dorney Lake. The much-maligned Dome would be used for indoor sports such as gymnastics and basketball along with the ExCel Centre in Docklands.

London's bid leaders also negotiated with the city's royal parks to host other events in temporary stadiums to be erected and then taken down once the Olympic flame had been extinguished. Greenwich would play host to the equestrian events, Hyde Park the triathlon and Regent's Park the road cycling.

The most daring use of London's landmarks, however, was to be the conversion of Horse Guards Parade in Whitehall for beach volleyball. The venue for the annual trooping of the colour and within easy viewing of Number 10 Downing Street, Horse Guard's would give a stunning backdrop to an already eye-catching sport and provide the Prime Minister with a hook for a well-received joke on his viewing habits. The London Eye and Westminster are all within view of the venue and for the television cameras it could be as memorable an image as Sydney's Harbour Bridge was during the hugely successful Games of 2000.

There were also sports to be held outside London – sailing would take place at the national yachting centre at Weymouth and Portland and the football tournament would be taken to venues throughout Britain.

It was an impressive vision for the Games and, as Sue Barker explained the plans to the audience, it was possible for the first time to really embrace how the London Olympics might look. It was an exciting moment for the whole bid team. 'Compact Games are what the IOC wants and this is exactly what this bid delivers,' said Cassani during her speech. Blair meanwhile made an impassioned appeal to the 117 IOC members who would eventually decide whether London should get the chance to turn the dream into a reality. 'I hope they give us the chance to host the world's most special sporting event here in the world's greatest capital city,' Blair told the audience. 'If they do that, I know we won't let them down.'

'Having the PM there was the key,' Lee says. 'He had not been in the rehearsals for the show so the plan was for me and Barbara to meet and greet him in his dressing rooms a few moments before it started. That was a vital moment for me because as the PM swept in he recognised me and asked how I was. Barbara could see immediately that there was a connection which would count going forwards.

'He asked us what we wanted him to emphasise but it was clear that he knew the brief. We gave him three points and he spoke without notes. He was superb.

'We were telling people new things and the messaging was working and, as I stood with Blair's head of communications David Hill and his Olympics adviser Sarah Hunter, we had the sense from a political point of view that the show was a success.

'Ken's speech was particularly powerful. He focused on London's diversity and the regeneration of the East End and said it could be a model for the rest of the world. He spoke passionately and people felt it. You always hold your breath with Ken but he was particularly impressive that day.

'These were important building blocks designed to counter claims that we did not have political support.'

As the show finished and the sports stars and journalists moved upstairs to mingle and indulge in a celebratory glass of wine in the Floral Hall, an impressive room with fabulous views over Covent Garden and beyond, Lee was convinced the show had been an even bigger hit than he had hoped. The sports exhibitions with the kids were a huge success and the one-to-one interviews with Cassani and other key players were all working. The international press reported how London had stolen a march on its rivals. New York's launch had been low key, emphasising how compact the 2012 Games would be in the Big Apple. NYC 2012's bid leader Dan Doctoroff said all venues would be within twenty miles of each other, with venues along bisecting lines in a giant X. The Olympic village would be at the midpoint, and athletes would arrive at the many venues via fast ferries.

'New York is a city like the Olympics – built on dreams,' Doctoroff said. 'Built on the idea of forming a single community of humanity, just like the Olympic Games.'

Paris, meanwhile, considered the city to beat, cited its successful hosting of the 1998 World Cup and the 2003 World Athletics Championships. 'We have the know-how of how to organise things on a large scale,' France's Sports Minister Jean-François Lamour, a former Olympic fencing champion, boasted to the audience gathered at the Eiffel Tower.

Meanwhile in Madrid, Prime Minister Jose Maria Aznar gave his full support for the campaign to bring the Olympics to Spain just twenty years after the Games in Barcelona.

'Madrid will be in the summer of 2012 the window from which all the world can see the amazing transformation taking place in Spain in the last decades,' Aznar said at the Moncloa Palace.

Similar events took place in Moscow, Leipzig and Istanbul. But it was London who came out on top for the first time. It was especially sweet for London to upstage Paris as a week earlier the Paris Mayor Bertrand Delanoe had publicly questioned the political solidarity behind London's bid. He had sneered: 'I cannot help but notice that the French consensus,

especially between Paris city authorities and the state, represented by the President of the republic, is stronger than that
between the mayor of London and the British Prime Minister.'

Delanoe's criticism, which was published around the world
by the French international news agency AFP, led to a warning
from the IOC's ethics commission which had set out tough
rules designed to prevent rival cities from criticising each other.
A month earlier the IOC had even warned Blair over what was
a relatively minor issue of mentioning the London bid at a
meeting of Commonwealth leaders in Nigeria.

The attack from Paris, however, raised the stakes and set the
tone for the rivalry that would underpin the race for the 2012
Games. With Anglo-French relations already strained over the
Iraq war, the 2012 campaign came to be viewed as a test of
the world status of Blair and the French President Jacques
Chirac.

To outdo the French was a major coup, especially as Lee
knew just how close the launch had come to going off the rails.
Just two days earlier, in a major drama, Cassani had raised
doubts about the likely impact and use of such a lavish launch
to the campaign and whether it would generate the necessary
interest. There was also the potential for embarrassment with
Blair and Livingstone together playing such high-profile roles.

Just days before the launch the Mayor of London had been
re-admitted to the Labour Party after being expelled four years
earlier for standing against the official Labour candidate in the
mayoral elections of 2000. Lee knew the political establishment and the press would be watching for any signals of unease
between the pair as they took their place on the same stage for
the first time since their fall-out. So, as the cameras trained
their lenses on the front row of the audience in the Royal
Opera House that day, Lee made sure the photographers
would not be able to get a shot of the two politicians away
from the main group.

'We had a problem with the photos because we couldn't
have the PM and Ken sitting next to each other,' said Lee. 'We
didn't want that photo becoming the story, but we knew there
was some value having them in a sort of group photograph. So
we set the front row up with the PM sitting next to Barbara.

Next to her on the other side was Tessa Jowell and right at the end of the group was Ken. It meant that Blair and Livingstone were never alone in the photographs.

'There were never any doubts expressed about them sharing a platform as this was a project where they shared the same vision, but we couldn't let their political history become the news story.'

The relationship between Blair and Livingstone became one of the most fascinating elements of the bid. Politically they were from opposite ends of the Labour spectrum and the media and public perception of their relationship was one of open hostility. But, in a revealing insight into the way the two men worked together before and during the London Olympic campaign, Livingstone explains that public perceptions can often be misleading. 'Just before he became Prime Minister I used to meet Tony once or twice a year for general chats,' he says. 'Once he became PM those meetings continued but, even before I left the party, they had to be kept secret. I used to be smuggled in the back door of Number 10 and told not to sign the visitors' register. But relations were fine and I had a good relationship with his main manager at the time, Angie Hunter, who was always a good link between us.

'Then you had this point where in the early summer of 2004, I had my first meeting with him since my re-election as mayor. I said to him that I would like to come back into the party and he was thinking about it. At that stage he genuinely suspected that the congestion charge wouldn't work and I would be a vote loser. So our relationship took a step backwards and went cold at that point.

'As the bid for the Olympics gathered pace I started having lots of meetings with him and the government again. It was the first time we'd worked together on a project other than just meeting to argue about what we didn't agree on. From then on he rapidly changed his mind and decided he wanted me back in the party.'

Blair backs up Livingstone's view of the relationship and added praise for the role he played during the campaign. He says 'I've always got on fine personally with Ken. It's pretty hard not to like him. But there's no doubt that working closely with him on the 2012 bid helped heal wounds quicker than might have been the case. Like so many people involved with the bid, he was fantastic.'

In their own contrasting ways Blair and Livingstone were absolutely crucial to the bid in those early days. Whenever Livingstone spoke about the regeneration of the East End or the multicultural nature of London he added enormous passion and credibility to the campaign. The bid team were aware of the potential pitfalls in allowing Livingstone to have such a high profile at times, but he was so crucial in showing London's commitment to the IOC that the risk was worth it. Blair, the smooth networker who brought so much political weight to the London bid, never let any differences with the mayor get in the way of the priority – giving London the best chance of winning the vote in Singapore. It is one of the remarkable by-products of the London campaign that it also helped bring the two politicians closer together.

'In my mind the success of the congestion charge was the most significant thing in mending our relationship,' believes Livingstone, 'but the bid did make a real difference and I think he found working with me was nothing like as difficult and as painful as he had been led to believe. People had been telling him I was mad, mainly people close to Lord Kinnock. Kinnock and I loathed each other because I was the only person back in 1992 who was telling him Labour couldn't win a general election with him in charge. I told him he should stand down but everyone else was telling him he could win. They coloured Blair's opinion of me but in the end we worked incredibly well together.'

One problem that would not be so easily solved, however, was London's transport system. It was a point of endless public and media debate and was most often seen as a potential major weakness in the London bid. And although the new Channel Tunnel Rail Link from King's Cross to Stratford would be finished in good time and guarantee a seven-minute trip from central London to the Olympic Park, the doubters focused on the general state of the transport system.

The tube was in clear need of updating, its signalling and track system considered to be out of date. The media pointed to the 'clean and efficient' Paris metro and said IOC members would never back London ahead of the French when it came to transport.

The IOC questionnaire submission was the first time the cities had been asked to submit any kind of transport plans. According to Lee, there wasn't a great deal of substance to tell them. He explained: 'We all knew going into that 16 January launch that there were big, big issues that needed to be addressed, particularly over the true level of political support. Public backing for the bid was still not great and the transport issue was very alive. The focus of the IOC transport question was very general and so was our answer.

'We still lacked a detailed transport plan for the Games and, as long as we were stuck on a debate about the general state of London transport, we were in trouble. It was a discussion out of our control.'

London would indeed be heavily criticised for their transport submission when the IOC reported back on the questionnaires in May. But, while transport became the number-one public priority for Lee to deal with, behind the scenes there was a much bigger problem brewing – the leadership.

It was not long after the January 2004 launch that Cassani began to have doubts about her own ability to front the campaign all the way to the vote in Singapore, eighteen months later. She had impressed people with her drive and energy but there were concerns beginning to grow over her relationship with ministers and ability to lobby key members of the IOC.

After the dust had settled on the Royal Opera House event and with the team basking in the afterglow, Mike Lee was shocked to discover that Cassani was not happy. 'Those of us who had been really clear of the need for this event felt vindicated. It had given us the most positive press since the bid really started. I had a sense that there was still a hell of a long way to go but we had got the best out of this particular milestone, both domestically and internationally.

'Amidst the public buzz around the event, however, there were some private doubts emerging. Maybe Barbara was already having her own reflections about whether she wanted to see the job through. There was more of a feel-good factor around the bid following the event – though no one was getting carried away. I argued that the success of the event had to be put into the context of where the bid was up to that point – it had been struggling. In my opinion there was not enough appreciation of what it had done in building some crucial credibility and helping to start changing people's perception of the campaign.

'I began to reflect myself on whether I had done the right thing by leaving UEFA. I wondered how long my relationship with Barbara would last and where we would end up under her leadership, given the scale of the challenges ahead.'

He would soon know the answer.

4. EXIT CASSANI

Barbara Cassani sipped her champagne and reflected on how far she had taken London's Olympic bid. It had developed from its tentative beginnings with no staff and no offices to the shortlist of candidates picked in May for the final International Olympic Committee vote in Singapore in July 2005. Considering how many people were writing the campaign off before it began there was a lot to be proud of.

It may not have been a perfect report from the IOC, but at least London was there. It was among the five shortlisted cities, ranked third behind Paris and Madrid but there were still fourteen months to close the gap. As Cassani stood beneath the London Eye on the capital's South Bank, chatting with guests and smiling, she knew it should have been a night for celebration.

More than five hundred people had turned out on a warm May evening to toast London's first major triumph on the road to the vote in Singapore. It was an occasion worthy of Hollywood: actors Sir Ian McKellen and John Hurt rubbed shoulders with sporting greats such as Sir Steve Redgrave and Sir Roger Bannister, the first man to break the four-minute mile.

'This is the greatest city in the world!' exclaimed McKellen, better known to many as Gandalf the wizard from the *Lord of the Rings* trilogy. 'It has always welcomed outsiders, immigrants, visitors. The heart of London is beating faster with the great news that we are on the shortlist – and about time too.

'If London is successful it will swell, and not just with pride. The East End will be revived with lasting sporting facilities. This is about feeling good about London and what it offers.'

And yet, on that sunny evening in May, Cassani didn't feel entirely good about London. She had sensationally decided to stand down as chairman of the 2012 bid team and the future was uncertain. At that moment only a handful of senior figures connected with the bid were aware of the bombshell news. It couldn't be made public for fear of causing irreparable damage to London's chances of being shortlisted by the IOC.

'I was made aware of Barbara's decision about a week before we went to Lausanne for the announcement on whether London had made the shortlist,' recalls Mike Lee. 'Barbara had told a small group of key people – there can only have been a handful who knew beforehand. That certainly included the Prime Minister, Tessa Jowell and Richard Caborn. Keith Mills was the first person she confided in, Craig Reedie and Ken Livingstone were also obviously in the loop. Seb Coe was aware of her decision to go but the issue of the succession was still to be fully sorted.

'Obviously it was absolutely crucial that this did not leak and everyone who knew was made aware of this. On the eve of being shortlisted by the IOC as a candidate city news of a bid leader's departure was potentially devastating.'

Few would have dared to doubt Cassani's enthusiasm for the project as IOC executives gathered at the Palais de Beaulieu Conference Centre in Lausanne on 18 May to consider their response to the bidding cities' questionnaires. In fact, on the day that the IOC was due to give its verdict on London and its eight other rivals, Cassani's name appeared on a thousand-word article in the *Daily Telegraph* in which she discussed the enormity of the task that lay ahead. 'The people of this country have entrusted us with their hopes and dreams, and we will not let them down,' she wrote. 'We owe it to our city and our country to succeed, but most of all we owe it to our children.'

These did not appear to be the words of a woman on the verge of resigning from the most important job on the bid team. It was true, of course, that she had failed to win over critics of her approach to the £150,000-a-year post. They still criticised the way in which she dealt with the male-dominated world of IOC lobbying.

So why did Cassani eventually decide to go? It seems she simply acknowledged that she wasn't the right person to deliver the bid. She could have tried to cling on and stomach the lobbying and travelling around the globe promoting the bid, but when it came down to it, it was not for her. She knew the time was right to hand over to someone else and she graciously fell on her sword.

'I was beginning to get suspicious that Barbara was starting to have some doubts in March,' recalls Lee. 'There was just a sense I was getting that she wasn't going to be in this for the long haul. There was a big debate going on in our international relations team, which was starting to map out the lobbying programme for the long slog up to the vote in Singapore. Questions were being asked about how much she was going to be involved in the travelling that would need to be done. She was indicating a reluctance to spend too much time on the road and in hotel lobbies and bars. My suspicions were confirmed when Keith Mills told me in confidence that Barbara intended to quit.'

Lee remembers two key aspects to the dramatic departure: first, the decision to hand the baton on to someone else having realised that she wasn't cut out for the role of leading the bid as it moved into phase two of the campaign; and secondly, her backing for Sebastian Coe to take on the job after she stood aside.

'Once it became clear that she wanted to go Barbara accepted that the key issue became her successor,' Lee says. 'She said the best man for the job was Seb but she didn't have any certainty of securing this. Seb might have been Barbara's nominee but there were lots of discussions going on behind the scenes about whether he was the right man. So a week before Barbara's departure would be made public the conversations about and with Seb had already started. I had private conversations with him but also with Keith, Craig and Tessa about it. For me, it also had to be Seb.'

But not everyone shared this view. According to sources there was a view within Labour party circles that a Tory peer such as Lord Coe was the last person they wanted to front Britain's £30 million bid for the Games. Lee said: 'There was a delay in immediately going with Seb and there was even a discussion in the culture department at one point about whether the job should be advertised and whether we should go to headhunters. At the time I also conceded to myself that in the long run I couldn't work for Barbara, particularly as I had become convinced we couldn't win with her as leader. On a day-to-day basis, my commitment to the bid and Barbara did not waver. However, I did feel it necessary to express some of my reservations and concerns to ministers. This was not an attempt to remove Barbara, rather to flag up some issues that might need addressing as the campaign evolved, particularly in terms of her management style and the needs of the international lobbying campaign.

'In the end the decision not to continue was Barbara's and I believe she took it in the best interests of the bid. It was a brave decision and whatever differences we had, I admire her for her courage.

'I shared the view that we needed to be decisive and that going through another lengthy selection process would sink the bid. We had fourteen months left to fight the campaign and we didn't have a moment to waste. Plus, in my mind, it was clear that Seb was perfect.'

But, as the IOC executive board meeting in Lausanne loomed large, so the delays continued. John Prescott, the deputy Prime Minister and bastion of old Labour in the Cabinet, was one who needed convincing. He was no fan of Cassani's and, at a meeting with the American and her Chief Executive Mills in March, he had been distinctly unimpressed. But now he would be faced with the prospect of the campaign being led by a Tory.

Richard Caborn, the Sports Minister and an old friend, was the first person to tell the fiery tempered deputy Prime Minister that the bid was suddenly in need of a new leader.

Caborn explained to Prescott that there was no time to readvertise the chairman's job and that Coe was perfect for the new phase the campaign was entering. The Prime Minister says he certainly had no doubts about giving the post to the Tory peer. Blair explains: 'I couldn't care less about him having worked for the Tory leader or his politics. You just knew he was the man for the job. I was just interested in his total enthusiasm for bringing the Olympics back to London, his experience and the impact he had on people across the world.' He and those select members of the Cabinet who were in the loop on Cassani's departure signed off Coe's promotion. There is no doubt in Lee's mind that these crucial days were central to the future success of the bid.

'I was driving home a few days before we were due to go to Lausanne,' Lee recalls. 'I was on my way to meet my wife for dinner in the San Daniele restaurant, in Highbury in North London. I remember pulling over to the side of the road and ringing Tessa Jowell and telling her "It's got to be Coe." She said, "I think you are right, but there are a few hurdles to clear yet." I knew the Prime Minister was comfortable but Tessa and Richard Caborn had to spend time persuading key players in the Cabinet. Over the weekend that followed I was in pretty constant contact with Seb, who hadn't even been officially asked about the job yet. I kept him updated on what was happening and he knew I was doing all I could to ensure he got the job. It also became clear that he was really up for it.'

By the Sunday before the bid team were due to fly to Lausanne for the IOC executive board meeting, the decision to appoint Coe as Cassani's replacement was a done deal. A lot of conference calls followed between all the key players to outline how they were going to handle the shortlisting and then a press conference the following day.

'We all knew it would be hugely damaging if it leaked out before the candidate city announcement,' says Lee. 'I don't think it was so significant that London would not have been shortlisted but we weren't prepared to take that chance. Everyone kept the secret and, as long as we kept it quiet, I was confident that the handover would come to be seen as a springboard for the rest of the campaign.

'It was a strange feeling when London's name was read out as one of the five who had made it. We had kind of taken it for granted that we would be, but when you were actually there it all became very tense. So, there was a massive sense of relief among all the members of the team. This was a historic moment in the bid but then we all knew that we had to prepare for something which could prove to be even more historic. Managing the media on this was undoubtedly one of the biggest challenges of my career.'

In a 106-page report prepared by an IOC working party, Paris, Madrid, London, New York and Moscow were the five cities chosen to go ahead to the final vote in Singapore. Havana, Leipzig, Rio de Janeiro and Istanbul were all rejected. Despite suggestions prior to the meeting in Lausanne that all nine cities might go through to the final round, the IOC knew dealing with all of them would be too cumbersome.

A special evaluation commission was to be set up to analyse each bidding city once they submitted their full bid books in November 2004. They were then to assess the documents before carrying out visits to each city in February and March 2005.

London and its four other rivals were still under strict new guidelines on bidding, but could at least begin planning to promote themselves at events around the world chosen by the IOC. It was to be a long hard road to Singapore involving thousands of air miles.

The sheer relief and delight of being chosen for the second phase of the contest was overshadowed for London, however, by the criticism the IOC made of their initial plans. The IOC report demonstrated just how hard the road ahead was likely to be. And it was transport that was to prove the biggest challenge to changing international perceptions of London as a city incapable of hosting massive global sporting events.

Although Cassani and her bid team tried to remain upbeat as London was announced as one of the shortlisted cities, they knew it was a damning report. It said: 'Rail public transport is often obsolete and considerable investments must be made to upgrade the existing system in terms of capacity and safety. Urban expressways and main arterial road facilities lack the capacity to provide reasonable travel times.' Claims of average bus speeds of 35mph also 'appeared unrealistic'.

The IOC comments placed massive pressure on the government and in particular the Transport Secretary Alistair Darling.

Cassani defended London against the IOC criticism of the transport plans saying that the situation had moved on a long way since the questionnaire was submitted in January. But she knew it was serious, and the team were very aware that more commitments would need to be secured to improve London's crumbling road and rail network. There was even talk that the £11 billion Crossrail project would have to be sped up to ensure it was ready for 2012.

'We did not get an easy ride from the IOC and the media,' Lee recalls. 'We were heavily criticised on transport and that was a problem. But we also knew that no proper work had been done on the detailed Olympic transport plan at this stage. The IOC questionnaire only required the most general information. I was sure that we could tackle the issue in the long run once some proper work was done on the transport plan.'

Although the IOC report ranked London above New York and Moscow, the city actually came top in only one of the eleven criteria, gaining joint first with New York and Paris for hotel accommodation. Some venues, situated away from the East London hub of the Games, such as tennis at Wimbledon, rowing at Eton and shooting at Bisley raised concerns about security as well as fears that competitors would spend hours in traffic jams. The IOC working party quoted its own independent survey, completed in January, which showed that only 62 per cent of the London public was in favour of staging the Games. There was also criticism that London's 'international sports experience is rather limited, with no world championships and few international sports events having been organised, with the exception of Wimbledon tennis and equestrian events'. The report pointed out that no new facilities were being built at that time, with the exception of Wembley, venue for the football finals, and, in addition, raised concerns about pollution levels in the capital.

Cassani's team responded positively to the findings and promised to learn lessons from the study. 'We are going to look at things,' she told journalists at the press conference in Lausanne after the IOC report was published. Lee was determined to move the story on. 'We briefed the media that venues might be reviewed to assess whether some more sports could be incorporated into the Olympic Park in Stratford. We also got the word out that there would be a press conference the following day in London which it would be well worth attending.'

But the message was clear: Paris, which scored 8.5 points under the IOC's marking system, which assessed and marked each of the key technical elements, was in front and it was their race to lose. Madrid, only 0.2 points behind the French capital on 8.3, was at that stage a better bet than London, which received only 7.6 points. New York was awarded 7.5 and Moscow 6.5. Cassani knew she was leaving the bid with an awesome task to come from third to win.

As Cassani and Lee boarded the plane back to London at Geneva, they both understood that her decision to quit as chairman could be perceived as a response to the negative findings by the IOC working party. Yet it was undoubtedly the right time to hand over to a new leader capable of taking the bid to the next level. Lee insists that the IOC report had nothing to do with Cassani's decision to quit. As for the gap, London would have to make up, he felt that once news of Coe's appointment filtered through to the IOC members and the bid began selling itself, it could make up the ground it needed to on Paris and Madrid.

He says that during that flight back to London Cassani showed no signs of regret at her decision to walk away. 'A lot of the team left Lausanne before Barbara and I did,' says Lee. 'They got an earlier flight but we had a lot of interviews to get through so we stayed to catch a later flight. The rest went back so they could be there for the start of the party at the London Eye.

'We discussed the day's events and her speech at the party. At Heathrow we were picked up by a car and driven straight to the event. Our plan was for Barbara to turn up once a speech by Ken Livingstone had finished. The idea was that the crowd would then turn to see Barbara and give her a hero's welcome.

'During the drive I was in constant touch with Fran Edwards, one of our senior press officers, but the traffic was very light so we got there sooner than expected. We had to drive around the Westminster area to allow Ken to finish. Once I got the message we pulled up and walked down towards the Eye. As Barbara appeared at the top of the ramp which leads down towards the entrance, the whole party – and remember there were around five hundred people there – turned to see her and let out a massive cheer. She was absolutely stunned by the reception. And for a moment I saw the hint of a tear in her eye. At that moment I think she had a full realisation of what she had done and, perhaps more importantly, that she was leaving behind this fantastic campaign.

'All credit to her, because, if she was thinking that, it was over in a flash. She went on to make a great speech and enjoy the party. No one appeared to sense anything major was about to happen. People were enjoying the fact that we had cleared the first major hurdle.

'I confirmed to the key journalists who were at the party that they should come to the press conference the next morning. There was a lot of intrigue but no one worked it out.'

But before Cassani went in front of the cameras the following day to hand over the post to one of Britain's greatest ever runners officially, another drama was to be played out. 'The following day was an incredible day,' recalls Lee. 'We were heading towards the lunchtime press conference and Keith called a meeting in the morning with all the bid's senior management to inform them what was about to be announced. I was focused on preparing for the conference and decided not to attend but I was told the meeting was stunned at the news. There was some anger and it was clear that there were several people very loyal to Barbara who just didn't want to accept that Barbara had resigned. However it was time to move on.'

Throughout Coe was kept informed of developments as he waited for the all-clear so that he could head for the press announcement. The press conference went smoothly. Cassani calmly delivered the bombshell news to a room packed full of astonished journalists who hurried off quickly to tell their news desks what had happened. Lee smiled, delighted that the news had remained secret until now and the handover had been accepted as smooth and logical.

Cassani told the conference: 'I am so proud of what we have achieved so far. My job has been to create a winning team and to develop an exciting blueprint for London 2012 – together with colleagues those goals have been reached. Our focus must now be on winning the support of the international sporting community and demonstrating London is the right choice for 2012. The changes in our organisation reflect these priorities. I am looking forward to working with Seb Coe, Keith Mills and the rest of the team to win that crucial vote in Singapore next July.'

Coe complimented Cassani saying: 'This is a great honour and a tremendous challenge. Barbara and the team have done a fantastic job in creating the building blocks for the bid. As a former athlete and Olympian, the Olympic Games profoundly and positively influenced my life. I want to give that opportunity to others and leave a legacy for future generations.'

'It was all remarkably upbeat,' Lee remembers. 'I think we did create a real sense of the baton passing over to Seb. And although most people know Seb for the two Olympic gold medals he won, he showed that there was a lot more to him that day than just being a sporting champion.'

The next day Coe left for the south-west for a tour of Devon, planned long before the bid's sudden change of leadership. It was decided to press ahead with the visit to show the new chairman getting down to work straight away. It was also an important visit to try to garner support for the bid outside the capital itself, a key aim at this stage of the campaign.

Although Lee admits he and Cassani didn't always see eye to eye on the direction of the bid under her chairmanship, he remains full of praise for what the London 2012 team achieved while she was in charge. Above all, she had assembled all of the key players who would go on and win the race for the Games, including Coe. 'The great thing about Barbara was that she was incredibly dynamic and focused as she built the team,' says Lee. 'In the early days when London 2012 was just starting out she created the whole thing from scratch. She made it surge ahead and if you look at the senior team involved in the final push in Singapore they had all been recruited by Barbara. In my opinion she just wasn't the person to lead that team to the end of its incredible journey.'

That was backed up by the PM who adds: 'We mustn't underestimate Barbara's role. She got the bid up and running and laid good, solid foundations for London's success. She deserves a huge amount of credit. But in the end, it was also right that she handed over the torch to Seb.'

What is absolutely certain is that Coe's sudden promotion gave the bid a massive injection of momentum at just the right time. With fourteen months to go one of the finest middle-distance runners the world has ever seen was in control of the race.

And, as a born champion, it was one he was determined to win.

5. READY ... STEADY ... COE

Even as a promising schoolboy, Sebastian Coe would train on Christmas Day. From an early age, Coe's father, Peter, had instilled in the future double Olympic champion an iron will which would serve him well throughout his hugely successful career. But, as Coe was to admit himself, the task of bringing the Olympic Games to London in 2012 was the most daunting challenge he had ever faced. He would need every ounce of that discipline and determination if London was to come from behind and beat the favourite Paris to the finishing line.

While it would be overstating it to claim that people thought London's bid was beyond hope in May 2004 it is certainly true that, outside of the bid team itself, there were very few people who genuinely believed it could win. Though the IOC had shortlisted London for the final round of voting in Singapore, the city was a distant third behind Paris and Madrid and had had major weaknesses in its transport plan highlighted. Added to that, bid leader Barbara Cassani had been replaced by Coe. It was a courageous decision. Seen in hindsight, of course, it was also an inspired one but at that point in the campaign very few observers thought his appointment would make a dramatic difference to the eventual outcome – defeat for London.

Coe never saw the race in such terms. He passionately believed London could win. More importantly he realised that this was a once in a lifetime chance for London to bring the world's biggest sporting event to Britain and one of his early messages to his staff was that 'there are no tomorrows'.

'This was a one-off window,' Coe recalls. 'This wasn't coming around again. I sensed halfway through this process, during the early days when things weren't easy, that there were suddenly some people saying, "if we are not successful". So I shut that down right away by saying if we are not successful this is not going to happen again. Firstly, the land is not going to be available in that shape or that scope. Secondly, you blow this with London and it isn't simply a matter of coming back in the water again. This is the best opportunity we have got because first of all if we don't win it Paris will and that means it won't come back to Europe again for a while. The next time there is a realistic chance of this baby coming around again is when I am in my seventies and frankly it's not something I want to do in my seventies.

'In a way it made us a better bid. I was determined that some time after Singapore we would not be sitting here saying, "Well, it was a bold, valiant and worthy attempt but we didn't get it. And we'll be here this time next year." I told people to forget all that. We were looking at young faces pleading with us to succeed in East London because the next chance we would get to bring the Games to that part of London would be when they were in their thirties. So it was very important for people to focus, and that brought out the best in all of us and me in particular. Whenever I felt it had been a long day and I wanted to shut my case and go home at 9 p.m., I thought, no. We are all a long time dead in this and if it doesn't happen, it's not going to happen again.'

In truth Coe had inherited a bid that had already assembled the key elements of a credible campaign. Cassani's great achievement, in particular, had been to kick-start the bid in its early days and assemble a highly motivated and immensely talented team, which was desperate for London to win. Now, under Coe, that team could start to flourish and begin the arduous process of selling London's vision to the IOC and the rest of the world.

As Coe says, 'We had a great senior team with the skills and commitment to win, but we needed to harness that team and really think through how we were going to win.' Coe was already a key player in that campaign – as one of three vice chairmen he played an important role promoting the bid, particularly outside London. His political experience as chief of staff to William Hague between 1997 and 2001 and before that as a whip in John Major's Conservative government while serving as MP for the Devon constituency of Falmouth and Cambourne was essential. In 2000 he was made a peer and entered the House of Lords.

But it was his credentials within the Olympic movement that made him such an important member of the bid team. Ever since he won his first gold medal in Moscow in 1980, he had been a favourite of IOC President Juan Antonio Samaranch. It wasn't just the fact that he had ignored a call from Margaret Thatcher's Conservative government of the day to boycott the Moscow Games, but also the nature of his victory on the track. Having lost the 800m for which he was favoured to his old rival Steve Ovett, Coe produced an extraordinary performance to beat him over 1,500m, a distance over which Ovett had not lost in 50 races. Four years later in Los Angeles he out-kicked Steve Cram to retain the 1,500m title, a victory which confirmed him as one of the all-time greats of middle-distance running.

Coe's easy charm and style had made a big impression on Samaranch and from that moment on he was earmarked for greatness and talked of as a future IOC member, and possibly even a President. Such was his popularity among the power brokers of the IOC that in 1988, when Coe famously failed to qualify for the Seoul Olympics, Samaranch tried to offer him a wild card so that he could attempt an unprecedented hat-trick of 1,500m Olympic titles. The move caused uproar and even Samaranch, the former Spanish diplomat, had to concede he couldn't just hand out Olympic invitations at will. Peter Elliott took Coe's place instead.

Sensing his standing in the IOC world, British sports officials fast-tracked Coe even though he was still competing. In 1986 he played a key ambassadorial role in the Birmingham bid for the 1992 Games, which were won by Samaranch's home city of Barcelona. After Birmingham's humiliation in the vote in Lausanne, one journalist recalls a conversation with a shattered

Coe in which Coe told him Britain would never again bid without London. But it would take two more failed bids from Manchester before the penny finally dropped with the rest of the British sporting establishment.

Coe says: 'I had been pretty disenchanted at our previous attempts to land this. They were worthy bids but a bit naïve and all the feedback from the IOC was, why don't you guys get serious about this? In fairness, London had some pretty serious issues to deal with. There was no strategic authority so there was no one organisation to sign for it and I know from my own experience that getting 32 London boroughs to think about anything uniformly is a pretty tricky business. Actually in 1980, the GLC put a feasibility study together on a London Games.

'There is a line I can remember in the 1980 film *The Long Good Friday* where Bob Hoskins is walking along the quayside with one of his police inspectors, who was on his payroll, and there is an exchange where Hoskins turns to him and says "Can you imagine doing the long jump along these quaysides in 1988?" The whole thing was based on converting the East End and, back then, it seemed so far fetched. London suffered in that period because there was no strategic authority thinking broadly about sport. Each of the boroughs did their own thing but cities like Manchester and Birmingham and Sheffield, because they were fairly stable local authorities at the time, were able to jump ahead. So there were some deep seated issues London had to confront.'

Despite his impeccable Olympic credentials, it took a long time for Cassani to make Coe a senior member of the bid team. Even then he was asked to do just one day a week and Coe, in his typically laid-back way, said he was too busy anyway. But it was a mistake that senior figures, especially Craig Reedie, insisted was put right.

'To be honest I slightly distanced myself from the whole process,' Coe says. 'I think Barbara was under some pressure to have a conversation with me. I'm not sure it was her natural inclination to ask me. I think it became a bit embarrassing and a bit of a problem. Every time I got phoned up by journalists I had to tell them nothing was going on and genuinely it wasn't. Then I can only imagine that the communications team were picking up on this and asking why I wasn't involved, and then we had a chat. I said to her, "Look I really believe we should go for this. I have made some high-spirited speeches in the Lords about this and I have pushed hard to get this off the ground."

'Some months earlier I had a discreet conversation with Craig Reedie and he and I were very open. We are extremely good friends and very close but there was a lot of talk of committees and I just instinctively recoiled at the thought of spending two or three years working in committee structures. I understand those structures and actually chair boards. But the reality is that, in a bid process, there are a handful of people who drive it through and they have to do that because there is no committee that can tell you how to deal with all the stuff that flies at you on a daily basis.

'So when I spoke to Barbara I was very open about it and said I was happy to play any role she wanted but it had to be properly choreographed. We then got to a position where she asked if I would like to be an ambassador and chairman of our celebrities and I said no. I didn't see my role in that way. But I told her if she wanted something more structured then fine. Then she came back with the offer of being a vice-chairman and I thought that the difference between that and being chairman was like president and vice-president, so it was a significant role and one I was very happy to take on.'

But when Cassani stepped down as chairman, Coe was suddenly thrust into an even more significant position – that of the leader. He was perfect for the role and, despite some doubts and concerns, his elevation to leader was eventually signed off. But while it is easy, with the benefit of hindsight, to look on his promotion as an obvious move, it still came as something of a surprise to Coe himself.

Coe explains: 'I remember the first time I sensed something could be changing was a few weeks before the shortlisting of the candidate cities. Keith Mills came up to me at a party at the Natural History Museum. He sidled up to me in one of the dinosaur galleries and said "Do you think it would be possible to give more time?" I said actually I've just done nine straight days. I don't think it's possible to give it more time but it is possible to do it smarter than the way we are doing it at the moment. At that time, one day I was in Cornwall and the next day I was off to engage with the international community somewhere overseas. I was all over the place.

'But I had no idea at that stage that his question was with a view to the change of leadership. That was some weeks before and then I heard nothing more from Keith. At that point I was a bit distant from the decision-making core of the bid. This is not a criticism of Barbara in any way because you do what you need to do and it's not always possible to engage with everyone you should.

'After that it was all very quick and these conversations were going on at some pace. Mike Lee and I talked privately but there was no formal approach until two or three days before it happened. To put it into perspective, I only spoke to the secretary of state on the Monday at the SportAccord event in Lausanne, just two days before the IOC meeting to announce the shortlisted candidate cities. At that stage Tessa said to me that Barbara Cassani wasn't going to continue in the chair and she asked whether I would take it on. I knew something might happen but was still surprised at how quickly it all moved.

'It was the neatest solution in hindsight and it was a solution which I am pleased was agreed. I think it would have been difficult if it had been a split decision but it had the support of all the key players: it was Barbara's suggestion, it had the support of the bulk of government although there were a few raised eyebrows about a former chief of staff in the Tory party suddenly taking this on. But, looking back, we weren't sitting there with the best deck of cards at this time.'

Coe is full of praise for the legacy Cassani left to him as he began the task of trying to win the 2012 Games for London. 'Barbara had done a sensational job in putting the start-up business together. There's no doubt about that one. When I first started talking to her in the September or October of the previous year, it was an empty glass box on the top of Canary Wharf. She did a terrific job in getting that started but at that stage it didn't have international credibility. It wasn't that the vibes were aggressive, it actually reminded me of election situations where you knock at the door, and the people you talk to are not angry, nor are they excited, they just aren't engaging. Internationally, the IOC members just weren't asking questions about it. It just wasn't on their radar screens as something that was remotely likely to happen. I never subscribed to the anti-American thing with Barbara, though I don't think it was the easiest thing and there was a slight feeling of, "Do you really need an American to run a British bid?"

'But if I am being honest I am not sure Barbara fully appreciated how hard this was going to be. That's not a criticism of her because you don't realise it until you do it. I have three friends who have been through this process, two successful and one not, and I know what they did and they put their lives on hold. But she was undoubtedly the right person to set up the business and drive it in those early stages.'

Behind the scenes and using his high-level contacts in government, Mike Lee made it clear that, in his view, Coe was the only realistic choice to replace Cassani. Despite coming from different political backgrounds, the pair had already forged a close relationship through sport, which relegated party politics to the background. 'I had actually worked with Seb some years before when I was working as a consultant to Seb's old university, Loughborough, who were bidding for the British Academy for Sport. We had several meetings and he was very supportive of the bid. I could see then that he had a great combination of his sporting background with good political understanding and he was obviously media savvy. I didn't meet up with Seb again until he became bid vice-chairman. But even then I could sense he was itching to play a bigger role. I could also sense that there was some tension between the bid vice-chairmen and Barbara. Yet even though his role was restricted in those days, we found ourselves agreeing on many of the big campaign issues.

'I found myself building a rapport with Seb. I have to make it clear that at no point was there any question of a conspiracy against Barbara but I knew we had to get him more heavily involved. On a personal level, I was delighted when Barbara indicated her intention to stand down and to nominate Seb as her successor. As we were looking at the needs of an international campaign, whatever doubts were expressed about Seb, for me he ticked all the right boxes. He was a great Olympic champion who had lived the Olympic dream. He is familiar with politics, he presents very well, he understands the media and so I felt not only could we work well together because of a common understanding of what was needed, but also because nobody could better represent London's Olympic aspirations.'

At this point in the campaign, taking on the challenge of leading London's bid was a risky one. Coe might have ticked all the boxes for Lee and his colleagues in the bid communications team, but it was a big risk for the Olympic champion. An embarrassing failure would see him held responsible and potentially hit any hopes he harboured of becoming a major player in the IOC. But he also had very strong reasons for taking it on. 'I thought I could make a difference,' he says. 'And I always thought that bringing the Games into your own backyard is such an unbelievable bridgehead into all the things I had spent most of my adult life promoting. More young people in sport, getting sport higher up the political and social agenda, the opportunity to repair the damage of industrial decline in one of the hardest pressed areas of this country, the opportunity to use sport to allow young people to fashion their futures through sport, the inclusion issue. All the things people heard me talk about forever and a day. Here they were and done properly there was an outside chance we could land this in the UK.

'We all have our own skills, but I actually thought there were a number of the skill sets needed here that were on my CV. I spoke to my closest friend, a former teacher who I have known for many, many years. He said of course I had to take it, there was no question, and if anyone could turn this around it was me. But he told me to bear in mind that at the end of this process I would either be carrying the torch or the can.

'I also had one or two conversations with my kids and I clearly warned them what could happen. I told them I would do what I could to see them and keep things normal but that I would have to do a lot of travel. But then halfway through this I remember talking to my youngest daughter, Alice, who was five years old at the time. Two weekends had gone already and I felt really guilty about it but then she said something to me that really was one of the nicest moments of the campaign. I said, "I'm really sorry. I know I've missed this and I've missed that and I'll make it up to you," but she looked at me and said, "It's all right, Dad, we want the Games." And I thought well, it's probably the only job I've done that kids understand. All the parents on the bid had the same reaction. It was the most extraordinarily talented team that have come together in pursuit of one objective like this.'

As Coe settled into the job of leading London's bid in the second half of May, both he and Lee knew the first few weeks would be a testing time. Coe would have to convince those who doubted his commitment to sport since his retirement from the track. 'I was aware of the reaction to me,' said Coe. 'But it was a classic British reaction from people in sport who can't understand why people want to go off and do other things. Anyone who knows how demanding it is to be chief of staff for someone like William Hague would never have questioned whether I had the commitment to do this. But then, the criticism wasn't really about commitment as far as I was concerned. It was really about why I had not chosen to live my life on the committee of the BOA. There is a level of nervousness in sport about people who choose to go on and do other things. The answer to those critics is simple. I never got fully engaged in sport because I didn't actually have the time to do it and didn't want to do something I couldn't give my full attention to.'

But support for Coe was not unanimous. With just over a year to go until the IOC vote in Singapore, an explosive resignation letter from London 2012 Project Manager Jane Willacy was leaked to *The Times*, accusing Coe of lacking the leadership needed to steer the bid in the right direction. A close ally of the sidelined Cassani, Willacy quit her job in anger after discovering her former boss had been reduced to working just one day a week in her new role as vice-chairman. In her letter Willacy claimed the campaign was directionless and driven by ego. She said the bid required a 'leader that will need to understand what needs to be fought for in a "winning" bid and the stamina and the guts to fight for it'. She added that she was 'concerned that individual agendas will be allowed to compromise the quality of the bid' and further claimed that already some senior staff were more worried about their own career path after the election of the 2012 host city was over.

Cassani's further removal from the centre of power wasn't the only issue at the centre of the dispute. Conscious of the criticism of London's transport plans six weeks earlier, Coe knew he needed an experienced operator who understood the specialised world of Olympic bidding, but his appointment of Australian Jim Sloman and his company MI Associates to the role of co-ordinating the detailed bid book to be submitted that November had also caused problems among the team.

'Jane was very loyal to Barbara,' recalls Lee. 'When Barbara was told she would only be doing one day a week this was widely interpreted as being marginalised. Jane Willacy's own position was highlighted and being discussed by Seb and Keith Mills. Because the team was looking at everything again under the new leadership, we decided we needed to raise the game on the candidate file. We lacked real experience of Olympic operations and we needed someone who could get to the heart of what the IOC and the members were looking for in a technical plan.'

One of Lee's team, Michael Pirrie, had links with Sloman, who had been the chief operating officer of the Sydney Olympics and was known to Coe and, once the connection was established, a decision was made by the bid leadership to ask Sloman and his company to come on board to re-energise the process of putting together the 600-page candidate file or bid book.

Lee says: 'Sloman was an important appointment for Seb. It showed first of all that he was prepared to make changes, it showed he was listening to advice and, for me, it confirmed what I thought: that his instincts were to win. Sloman and his team set in motion a review of the existing technical plans and brought to it a real edge in terms of what would work and what the IOC needed and wanted to see.

'Sloman also helped to bring new focus to the transport issue by working with Transport for London, ensuring that the work concentrated on delivering a four-week transport plan rather than a general review of the whole of London's infrastructure. This was crucial because it allowed us to begin to move away from a general debate about transport, and the impact of the Northern Line breaking down on a wet Monday morning, and to focus on things like Olympic lanes, Games traffic flow, and passenger management and the high-speed Channel Tunnel rail link.'

Lee had to use all his PR skills to ensure the Willacy email didn't blow the bid off course just as it was beginning to show signs of real promise. 'It was certainly the time for some fire fighting,' he recalls. 'It had the capacity to open up a lot of wounds. It was important to dampen all that and make it clear that changes had been made in the best interests of the bid. To read that email would make you believe that the bid was in disarray, that Barbara had been badly treated, staff morale was low and that people were only interested in their careers. But as it turned out it was a temporary blip because we shifted the focus and used the episode to demonstrate the decisiveness of Seb with the announcement of the appointment of Jim Sloman and his team.'

Coe's shrewdness was just one of the qualities Lee would become familiar with over the next twelve months of the campaign. The two men grew increasingly close and developed a real sense of trust. That didn't stop Lee from falling victim to the London 2012 chairman's sense of humour, however.

'Seb's good fun to be with,' he reflects. 'Most people only see the serious side but he has a really wicked sense of humour, which can sometimes be slightly terrifying for a communications director. One time we were in Dubrovnik for the gathering of all of the European Olympic Committees. It was a very important presentation. We had three pretty intensive days of work and on the final evening after all the work was done the team went out to celebrate. We went to a restaurant and a few bars and we ended up in a Dubrovnik nightclub with a bar and a dance area which had poles and a stage. I was in the bar area chatting with various people, when suddenly Debbie Jevans, one of the key players on the international campaign team, came running in and saying, 'Mike, Mike . . .

you must come quickly. Seb's clearly out of it and is up on stage doing a pole dance and there are a load of journalists and a photographer in there. Can you come and sort it?'

'So I immediately went into PR mode, put down my beer and rushed into the other room. As I did this, Susie, Seb's PA, gave Seb the nod and he leaped up on stage and writhed around one of the poles, popping his shirt buttons. I immediately went into autopilot, charging around the bar trying to find the journalists, ready to do all I could to stop the story, with Seb making increasingly provocative gestures on stage. Then, all of a sudden, he stopped and winked at me, and the whole room burst into laughter. I still haven't got him back for that.'

Despite that scare, Lee knows the decision to appoint Coe was an inspired choice. 'Seb is not noted for his micro management,' he said. 'But what he did was provide leadership and encourage those around him to develop a winning strategy. He built a new team spirit and also showed he was prepared to lead from the front.'

With the right leader in place and the London team rejuvenated under Coe, the bid stepped up a gear. Within a year they would be in Singapore for the big vote. There was much work to do and so little time. Having formed the basis of a potentially successful Games plan, it was now time to hit the road and sell the London dream. The next twelve months would be a blur of hotels and airports. Coe put his previous life on hold and prepared to chase down the leader Paris, starting on the crucial battleground of the Athens Olympics. It was not long, however, before he was facing the biggest crisis of the whole campaign.

6. TO ATHENS – MAKE OR BREAK

S eb Coe was putting the finishing touches to a detailed plan
of lobbying to be carried out during the Athens Olympics
when a copy of London's *Evening Standard* was dropped on to
his desk at bid headquarters in Canary Wharf. Coe glanced up
from his paperwork to see Mike Lee standing in his office.

For once, the communications director did not say a word
to his boss. But there was a look of serious concern in his eyes.
As the two men looked down at the headline on the back page
in front of them they shared a knowing look. The *Standard*'s
headline from 9 August 2004 made depressing reading: 'LON-
DON 2012 BID HIT BY BACKLASH'. The story went on to say
how London's bid had been 'brought to its knees' by a TV
programme to be aired by the BBC.

Coe and Lee knew they were about to face the biggest crisis
of the 2012 campaign. They would need to use every bit of
their political and Olympic expertise to try to rescue the bid
from an early death. Tony and Cherie Blair, Kelly Holmes and
the 'great British sport-watching public' would all be called
upon to help save the campaign.

The Athens Olympics were to turn into what Mike Lee calls
'make or break' for the London bid. Reporters who had
travelled early to Athens for the International Olympic Committee meetings before the Olympics did not need to talk to
IOC members for very long before the word '*Panorama*' was

dropped into their conversations with a heavy thud. The BBC's current affairs *Panorama* programme 'Buying the Games' had secretly filmed four Olympic 'agents', who claimed they could secure the votes of IOC members for cash. The sting, which involved reporters posing as a bogus East London business consortium, had been broadcast the previous week. It had already had a huge impact on the IOC.

The cover story was simple but credible. *Panorama* reporter Justin Rowlatt had travelled around the world pretending to be the head of a company called New London Ventures. The firm were consultants working with clients with business interests in East London, who, for their own commercial interests, wanted to see the 2012 Games come to London. Rowlatt had talked to one 'Olympic agent' who said bidding was all about money. He said up to £1.9 million would be needed for between 15 and 20 votes – plus an agent's fee of nearly £600,000.

IOC members who had either seen the programme or heard rumours about it were furious. Firstly, the allegations had brought back memories of the 1999 Salt Lake City corruption scandal when ten members were forced to leave the IOC. The IOC was still struggling to clear the smell of corruption which had dominated its coverage in the international media with members accused of turning Olympic bidding races into 'freebie fests'.

The *Panorama* programme had dug up the whole affair again. The last thing IOC members wanted, on the eve of the Athens Games, was another scandal. What was far more damaging for London's bid, however, was the BBC's under-cover operation – hidden cameras and microphones and the bogus organisation.

Few Olympic leaders arriving at the Hilton Hotel in Athens and taking their first drinks on the balcony of the Galaxy Bar at the top of the building, were discussing the spectacular view of the ancient Acropolis in front of them. *Panorama* was far more important. Many were saying that they would be deeply wary of future contact with British officials.

One member said: 'For London officials trying to make contact with IOC members, it is going to be like having the plague. If there was a vote tomorrow, London would not get past the first round of voting. It's a knockout punch in the first round for London and it is going to take a massive PR effort to get the bid off the floor.' Even IOC members known to be strong supporters of London's bid were writing off the capital's chances. This was the London team's worst nightmare. The most important aspect of Olympic bidding is gaining the trust and confidence of IOC members. This is far more important than the pages and pages of technical plans and promises which bidding cities provide to the IOC. Although London 2012 were putting together a sophisticated bid book of plans for the Games, the team knew the promises were largely worthless if members did not trust them to deliver.

'*Panorama* was certainly a serious blow to the bid,' recalls Mike Lee. 'It had the potential to cause us more damage than anything else. We knew the potential scale of the backlash. Weeks before there had been rumours at bid headquarters that *Panorama* was making a programme about the Olympics. But it was not clear what it was going to be about. We put some feelers out with some of our contacts in the BBC. But there is always a firewall constructed around *Panorama* programmes and it is incredibly hard to find out what they are doing.

'Then we discovered that it was an undercover operation. It was not long before *Panorama* made direct contact with Keith Mills and me. Their questions did not reveal what they had done and I was shocked when I found out that they were acting as London representatives. But we understood that the pro-gramme was largely in the can and our plan had to be to minimise the damage.

'We knew that the undercover operation would not be appreciated in certain countries where that kind of journalistic tactic is illegal. We also knew that abroad the BBC was seen as a state organisation and many people wouldn't be able to understand how the government had allowed the programme to be made. Of course that level of control can't and shouldn't exist in our country. But we had to deal with that perception among the IOC members and the potential impact on the bid.'

The issue of trust was no different from the world of business or politics where personal relationships are crucial to any sale, contract or alliance. When former IOC President Juan

Antonio Samaranch had taken charge of the body at the 1980 Moscow Olympics, few cities were ready to accept the financial burden of the event after watching Montreal citizens take on huge debt to host the 1976 Games. One of his biggest successes in the 1980s and 1990s was to improve the financing of the Olympic movement through sponsorship and TV rights deals, which meant that an array of cities were desperate to stage the event.

But the increasing commercialisation of the Games meant that, inevitably, there was more at stake for the bidding cities. Before the rules on contact with IOC members were restricted following the 1999 Salt Lake City scandal, officials from bidding cities would take members to their favourite golf courses, football clubs or theatres in an effort to win friends and influence people. Lavish receptions and trips would be put on for IOC members and their spouses when they visited bidding cities. Officials from candidate cities put together detailed lists of the favourite activities and tastes of IOC members and their spouses and they would spare no expense in making sure Olympic leaders felt at home when they were in town.

The lure of cash or a free operation or education for a son and daughter abroad had certainly tempted some into crossing the moral line. In some parts of the world this kind of 'greasing the wheels' was part of doing everyday business, but the IOC holds itself up as a guardian of fair play and ethics. Its moral credibility for punishing competitors who cheat – with drugs or by breaking other rules – was undermined by the Salt Lake City scandal. The problem for IOC members was that they were all being tarred with the same brush.

It was an easy cliché to roll out for commentators who had never been near an IOC gathering – 'corrupt IOC members constantly on the gravy train'. Whatever the reality, perception was crucial and the IOC could not tolerate a reopening of this wound.

Salt Lake City got caught offering favours because officials kept detailed files of the gifts handed out to IOC members. When veteran Swiss IOC member Marc Hodler made the issue public, the scandal suddenly became international news and it was not long before the IOC had to act. In effect the cities bidding for 2012 were not even allowed to buy a cup of coffee for an IOC delegate during the 2012 bidding race. Coe and his team had to rely on 'meeting IOC members by accident' at conferences and sports events.

So, given the new restrictions, Coe and his team saw the *Panorama* programme as a brutal kick in the teeth. Contact with IOC members was already difficult enough without members worrying whether the officials from London talking to them had cameras hidden in their bags.

IOC members also saw this as a harsh reminder of the tough British media. While the French media was largely backing the Paris bid in cheerleading mode, it was clear that even those British newspapers that supported the campaign were going to criticise London 2012 along the way. Britain has some of the most active and inquisitive newspapers in the world. Some IOC members feared that they would have seven years of hassle from the UK media if they handed the Games to London. Paris was a much easier option, in that respect.

Lee and Coe did everything they could to soften the blow of *Panorama* and to stop it becoming a massive story. Lee explains: 'Before we went to Athens, Seb and I went to see the BBC Head of News, Richard Sambrook, to see how the programme would be handled. We knew the BBC *News at 10* often gave *Panorama* investigations high profile in their Sunday night broadcast. How the BBC presented the programme could be just as damaging as the programme itself. We also had high-level contact with Chairman Michael Grade and Director-General Mark Thompson. Of course, we understood that the BBC is an independent news organisation but we made certain pleas about how the programme would be handled. There was a real danger that it could be over-hyped and made even more damaging.

'In the end we weren't allowed to see the programme before it was broadcast. So Seb, Keith Mills, Craig Reedie and I decided to have a conference call from our homes immediately after it went out on the Sunday. There was a certain amount of relief that it was not as devastating as had been suggested – for us or the IOC.'

Nevertheless, the senior team knew that there was a serious danger that the programme could have a very negative impact on the bid. Coe knew that the full extent of the damage would only become clear when all the IOC members started arriving in Athens. As news of the programme spread around the IOC's global village, London's friends in the Olympic movement started to send back the bad news to headquarters at Canary Wharf. When the *Evening Standard* dropped on his desk, the double Olympic champion realised that his worst fears had turned into reality.

Lee says: 'We realised then that Athens was going to be a watershed. It was make or break for the bid. We had been through some serious ups and downs in the previous months with Barbara Cassani's departure, Jane Willacy's leaked email and the static level of public support for the bid. We had taken a few blows and we knew Athens would be crucial. Yet we were heading to Greece feeling very vulnerable. *Panorama* had the potential to do serious damage to the campaign. Our rivals also knew this. It soon became clear that some were basking in our difficulties around the show. They were going around saying that we were a very wounded bid – a boat that was sinking fast.'

As one of the first senior London 2012 representatives in Athens, it was up to IOC member Craig Reedie to start bailing out the water. The Scot immediately tried to calm the nerves of fellow IOC members by telling them that he had written to BBC Director-General Mark Thompson complaining about the programme. The letter asked how the broadcaster could criticise the Olympic movement so soon after buying the exclusive rights for the Games for the next seven years. It also attacked the undercover reporting tactics used by the programme: 'I believe they are legal, although questionable, in the UK but not legal and considered offensive in many countries. You will not be surprised to hear the reaction in the IOC is one of considerable irritation.'

But it was clear that much more than a letter was going to be needed to calm IOC concerns and fears. As the bid team touched down in Athens, they realised that one of their first tasks was to distance London 2012 from the *Panorama* programme. It was also important to stress to IOC members that the British media could be an asset, rather than a problem. Preparations for the 2000 Sydney Olympics had been covered by an equally aggressive Australian media and yet the Games were the best organised and best attended in the history of the movement. The Australian media had kept the organising committee on their toes throughout the seven years of preparation for the Games. Every decision was closely analysed, every mistake highlighted.

An inquisitive media is not necessarily good for the physical and mental health of the chief executive of an organising committee and many do not last the full seven years. However the close monitoring can make for better Games. If the organising committee of the 2004 Athens Olympics had faced an Australian or British media on a daily basis, it is extremely unlikely that Greece would have been allowed to get so far behind in their construction of venues.

Greece's last-minute scramble to get ready for the Games – a huge international media story in the months before the Games – was no longer the main talking point in the Divani Caravel Hotel in Athens, where the IOC's Session, the organisation's annual general meeting of all members, was taking place in the days before the opening ceremony.

Keith Mills bid Chief Executive recalls: 'Every member I talked to said we were dead. They couldn't understand why the BBC wanted to do this having just won the TV rights for the Games. They couldn't understand how the government could have let it happen on a state broadcaster. And entrapment was also illegal in some countries.'

The *Panorama* programme found its way on to the agenda of both the meeting of the IOC's ruling executive board, the 'Olympic Cabinet', and of the full IOC Session. IOC President Jacques Rogge was determined that talk of corruption was not going to dominate the build-up to the Games. He had already viewed a tape of the programme and passed the whole case over to the IOC ethics commission, the body responsible for policing the behaviour of IOC members and bidding cities.

Juan Antonio Samaranch junior, the son of the former President, then brought up the issue at the IOC Session and asked for an urgent screening of the programme for IOC members in a room. At the time Samaranch's move was interpreted by some as exacerbating London's woes and spreading the negative publicity around the programme though Samaranch denied this vehemently when questioned by reporters in the lobby of the IOC hotel.

It is hard to say whether there were political games being played on the fall-out from *Panorama*. There were plenty of conspiracy theories doing the rounds in Athens. But the Spanish financier was later to play an important role in helping London win the Singapore vote, once Madrid was out of the contest and, with Paris regarded as the clear front-runners, it was probably not in Madrid's interests for London to be destroyed.

The wider airing of the programme did have an upside for London. Lee explains: 'We had mixed feelings about Samaranch's request. We felt that it would give the programme an increased profile, which of course we didn't want. On the other hand, we knew there were a lot of misconceptions out there. Some people had the idea that we had collaborated on the programme and that we had even been involved in the undercover operation. So a full broadcast of the programme could help clear the air on that.'

Coe and Lee, both dressed in dark suits and ties despite the sweltering heat outside, stood nervously with their senior colleagues in the hallway of the Divani Caravel Hotel as around fifty IOC members made their way from the IOC Session to an early-evening screening of the *Panorama* programme in a private room.

This was all about a 'damage-limitation exercise'. And not just for London 2012. Giselle Davies, the IOC's communications director, did not take long to join the group of journalists waiting with Lee and Coe to emerge from the screening. There was a certain irony in her situation. The IOC spin doctor's father, Barry Davies, has spent most of his career at the BBC commentating on football, Olympic Games and major public events and is one of the corporation's household names. As a thirty-something woman who regularly travels from IOC headquarters in Lausanne to her London flat for long weekends, Giselle Davies had to be seen as completely neutral in the 2012 race –especially by the French media. She was helped in that goal by her ability to speak fluent French. Now, here she was facing a potential spat with one of Britain's most important institutions and having to make sure the programme's allegations did not hurt the IOC.

As the IOC members made their way into the room, Coe simply greeted as many people as he could with a smile and a firm handshake. He knew the real talking had to be done when they left the viewing. The IOC delegates were expected to discuss the programme among themselves and digest its findings, before emerging to face the media.

Coe and Lee talked nervously with journalists for the following forty minutes or so while the members watched the tape. Lee was desperately trying to put a positive spin on the affair. It was important that he did not give away his true fears about the damage it was causing. Coe and Lee had to give the impression that the bid was not panicking. This was not too hard for either of them. A former MP and seasoned PR man are used to the odd bit of theatre.

Lee explains: 'We had devised an action plan for the foyer. Seb and Keith Mills were concentrating on the IOC members, Craig Reedie was working it from the inside and my job was to talk to as many of the reporters as possible. Seb did a lot of listening when the members came out. He wanted to gauge the scale of the reaction and to reassure them that the London bid was not involved in the making of the programme in any way.' The view of many of the delegates after the screening was that they could see that the bid was not involved in the programme or its tactics. Coe's goal had been to put as much water between the bid and the programme as possible. The screening had clearly helped him to do that.

After speaking to as many members as possible and then doing a few interviews with the reporters, Coe appeared to breathe a sigh of relief as he left the hotel to begin the five-minute walk up to the Hilton Hotel with Lee. Both men were looking forward to an early-evening beer and a decent dinner after a difficult start to their Athens assignment. But the London team knew that the bid was far from out of the woods on this issue. There would still be plenty of suspicion among the IOC members about both the British media and new figures appearing on the IOC scene claiming to be representatives of the London bid. The *Panorama* programme had made it even more important that every IOC member dealt with London 2012 figures they knew and trusted. This would mean Coe, Craig Reedie and Keith Mills would have to do most of the travelling around the world to Olympic events in the next twelve months, whether they liked it or not. Debbie Jevans, the sports director, would also be important. She was a known quantity among the presidents of international sports federations having worked for the International Tennis Federation and the International Rugby Board. London had always planned to be a bid of 'familiar faces'. But it became even more important after *Panorama*.

Lee says: 'After the screening we felt we had managed to limit some of the damage. But there is no doubt that it was all still capable of haemorrhaging again.'

The next morning Coe, his assistant, Susie Black, and Lee sat in the café on the ground floor of the Hilton Hotel, reflecting on the previous day's events and looking out through the large windows at Greek policemen controlling heavy traffic on a blistering hot day. The aroma of fresh coffee filled the cool, air-conditioned room. With the traffic noise muffled by thick double glazing, the only sound to disturb the peace was the odd clink of spoons on saucers behind the breakfast bar where the staff prepared drinks to be served in the spacious lobby.

The tranquillity contrasted sharply with the madness outside as Greece rushed to get everything ready to open the biggest sporting show on the planet. For Coe, this was also a rare moment of calm before the storm. London's bid leader knew there were three weeks of hard work ahead. The Athens Olympics was one of the first major occasions when contact was allowed between bidding cities and IOC members. London's bid team had a massive job on their hands to win friends and votes.

London's opponents were already in town in huge numbers. Philippe Baudillon, the shrewd former diplomat who led the lobbying team of the Paris bid, had already been spotted regularly in the marble surroundings of the Hilton Hotel lobby. Jon Tibbs, the British public relations expert who had been signed up by the French to deal with the international media, was also a frequent visitor to the hotel, regularly chatting with the small group of 'IOC beat' journalists who would gather in the lobby to snatch a few words with IOC members. Rumours were also rife that another Briton Iain Macleod, a former *Daily Telegraph* journalist-turned Olympic bid consultant, was about to join the French campaign.

Macleod and Tibbs are two of the best-known consultants in the Olympic world. They were both involved in Beijing's successful bid for the 2008 Games in 2001. Tibbs first made his mark as one of the international public relations advisers for Athens during its successful campaign for the 2004 Games in 1997. In his early forties, the former rugby player from Kent only knew what it was like to win an Olympic bid. He had yet to lose a Summer Games campaign and had used this experience to build close links with the international PR company Weber Shandwick.

Macleod, a no-nonsense Scot who grew up in the remote island of Lewis in the Outer Hebrides, also enjoyed good contacts with the key international journalists and opinion-formers in the Olympic world. But his main expertise was as an 'information man' who gathered the latest views of IOC members and turned them into reports for bidding cities.

Macleod, who lives in the scenic Swiss 'Olympic capital' of Lausanne where the IOC is based, is very rarely quoted in newspapers or on television. He works very much behind the scenes and can often be found late at night in deep conversations around the bars and lobbies. At fifty, he is one of the Olympic consultants who aspire to analyse the IOC on various levels and understand the 'three-dimensional political chess' played by the members of the organisation.

Tibbs and Macleod had been keen to work for London and had provided advice and reports free of charge to Barbara Cassani in the early days of the bid. But neither had really hit it off with the American businesswoman and both had failed to come to any agreement to work for London. They were quickly snapped up by Paris, who had decided for the first time to broaden their horizons and look for expertise from outside of France.

Both men were formidable opponents for Coe's bidding team. But there was another 'Olympic networker' regularly roaming the Hilton Hotel lobby and bar who was even more dangerous to London – a shrewd 63-year-old American lawyer called Charlie Battle. Battle had been involved in Atlanta's shock victory in the race for the 1996 Games. He was widely regarded as one of the best Olympic lobbyists in the business and was part of the New York 2012 campaign. He had been lobbying IOC members for years. Like a seasoned diplomat, he has a brilliant ability to remember the names and lives of anybody he meets. Always well dressed, Battle's southern American drawl is well recognised in the IOC. His job in the 2012 campaign was to introduce Dan Doctoroff, the deputy mayor of New York and the key figure in the New York campaign, to as many Olympic personalities as possible.

On paper they had a hard task on their hands because there was still a great deal of anti-American feeling in and around the IOC. Many members had not forgiven Salt Lake City, and the 1996 Atlanta Games had suffered from serious problems with transportation and technology and a general over-commercialisation of the event. Yet it is a credit to Battle's skills that, despite these hurdles, it was widely believed in Athens that Havard-educated Doctoroff was doing a brilliant job at turning around the views of IOC members.

With the French and Spanish IOC members also working hard for the Paris and Madrid bids, Coe knew his lobbying team would really have to lift its game to new levels.

Lee admits: 'In footballing terms, we went into the Athens Games two goals down after *Panorama*. But we had a plan to get out of trouble and bounce back into the game. We knew that we had the advantage that Tony and Cherie Blair would be coming to the Games and meeting IOC members. We also had a unique plan to take our campaign away from the lobby of the Hilton Hotel. We wanted to meet IOC members in their natural environment – watching their favourite sports at the Olympics.' They had realised that it is hard to start up a conversation in a hotel lobby but, with sporting action going on, the small talk comes easy. Lee felt the bid 'had been bruised by *Panorama* but we were determined to get back on our feet'.

The British embassy in Athens is a short walk away from the Hilton Hotel, just off the Leof vas Sofias main road which runs into the centre of the city. From the outside it looks like a fortress. The street beside the entrance to the building is closed off to traffic and full of concrete blocks designed to stop truck bombings. High fences, armed guards and CCTV cameras surround the complex, which also contains the ambassador's residence. The German embassy on the other side of the street has no such high-profile protection. But the British have been worried about terrorist threats long before the Iraq war. In 2000 the embassy's defence attaché Brigadier Stephen Saunders was assassinated on his way to work by Greece's November 17 terrorist group.

Once visitors have made their way through the tight security checks, the building does offer some charm, however. It is a perfect place for an outdoor drinks reception. The business end of the building is equipped with modern air-conditioned offices. The ambassador's side of the complex enjoys the luxury of a walled garden with plenty of shade on hot summer days. It was on this small, protected piece of British soil in the Greek capital that the London 2012 bid began a remarkable comeback in the race for the Games.

Drinking British tea in china cups and nibbling at Greek croissants, the bid team held a planning meeting at 7 a.m. every morning at the embassy, away from the gaze of their rivals. The exact movements of every member of the lobbying team throughout the day were planned, the media plan of the campaign was discussed and the feedback from meetings with IOC members was analysed.

In the garden outside, Tony and Cherie Blair made their first entrance into the strange world of Olympic lobbying. Although it was not publicised for security reasons, the Blairs' trip to Athens had been planned for nearly a year. They had arranged their family summer holiday around the Games. The Prime Minister was unable to attend the whole of the event but the plan was for Cherie Blair to spend a lot of time in Athens during both the Olympics and Paralympics. Before the opening ceremony, the Blairs attended a garden party at the embassy held for Commonwealth IOC members and Sports Ministers, many of whom had been involved in a meeting with Sports Minister Richard Caborn earlier in the day.

'Tony and Cherie worked that garden party beautifully,' recalls Mike Lee. 'The whole event created a good image and showed the level of government commitment. The word soon got out in the IOC that the Blairs were in town.'

It was also at the embassy that a series of one-on-one meetings were arranged by BOA Chairman, Craig Reedie with the Prime Minister and a select group of influential IOC members. The meetings were kept secret. These one-on-ones would become even more important in the final days before the vote, but in Athens the London team learned that *Panorama* was clearly still a big issue. Members were asking the Prime Minister why he hadn't done anything to stop the programme. He had to explain that the BBC was an independent organisation and it was not for the British Prime Minister to stop a programme like that being broadcast.

Lee recalls: 'The Blairs also went out to visit the athlete's village with BOA chief executive Simon Clegg. The Prime Minister saw for the first time what is basically a global village with athletes and officials from all over the world. We made a short video with him from the village, which was later shown to the media in Athens as part of London's first major presentation to an international audience. He was unable to attend the presentation but we were able to show that he had been at the heart of the Olympic village.

'Then the Prime Minister and his wife went to the opening ceremony at the Olympic stadium, the only political leader from the five candidate cities to attend. He and Cherie looked so alive with the whole event. Their sheer joy watching the parade of teams made for great TV pictures, which were broadcast around the world. Their presence also made a clear statement to the IOC that the government was serious in its support of the Games and the bid. It was a defining moment for us.

'There is no doubt that Tony Blair was inspired by the Athens Games. He saw for the first time, first hand, how the Olympics can capture the imagination of a country and how they can bring about massive change. He witnessed the huge scale of the event and could see that Athens had changed dramatically in the run-up to the Games. In addition to the sports facilities, the city boasted a new modern airport, many new roads and a series of recently constructed underground and tram lines. Many of its hotels had been renovated and, despite the rushed preparations at the end, the Greek nation was immensely proud to be putting on the Games.

'Tessa Jowell told me that the Prime Minister went back to Britain with a renewed enthusiasm to do everything he could to bring the Olympics to London.' Tony Blair himself explains: 'It was important because I saw just what the Games meant and what it could do for a city. It made me realise just what a prize it was and how we must try everything we could to win it. With hindsight, I think it was also important for the IOC that Tessa and I went. It helped them realise that the UK wasn't just going through the motions but were absolutely serious about bringing the Games to London.'

Yet, despite the success of the Prime Minister's visit at the start of the Games, the 7 a.m. strategy meetings at the embassy were still having to focus on the aftershocks of *Panorama*. The lobbying team had to work harder.

With the action under way all day at the Games, the London 2012 team began its plan to take the 'lobbying away from the lobby' and into the sports venues. The movements of Coe, Mills and Reedie were organised with a detailed schedule between 8 a.m. and midnight so that they could get to as many sports venues as possible where they could mix with IOC members in the VIP boxes and in the Olympic hospitality suites. Coe did not worry that this left the Hilton Hotel free for London's rivals to roam because most IOC members would only make their way back there late in the evenings.

Lee explains: 'We wanted to be seen to be engaging with sport and the lobbying team made that their focus. London had the advantage of having an Olympic champion at the head of its bid and it was better to be out where the action was happening, rather than hanging about at the hotel. Seb and Keith went to every one of the 28 sports. They met a high proportion of members in the Olympic family lounges. The plan was not necessarily to talk about the bid but just to make friends.'

When Cherie Blair returned to Athens later in the Games she joined the campaign trail and was also often seen at venues chatting to IOC members. The Prime Minister's wife was impressed by London 2012's lobbying operation.

She recalls: 'My first realisation came there that we really did have a great team. It was a very slick operation. I had always been enthusiastic about the Olympics and, never having experienced before the way people came together, you could just see the potential and how we could do it so well in London. There was a lot of latent support for London, some of it because of 1948 and the way London stepped in after the War, this was particularly important among some of the older members.

'There was still some hesitation about our support for America and the Iraq War and then there was a genuine concern about whether we really meant it and whether we were going to do it half-heartedly. And there's no doubt at all that there was concern about the media. It wasn't helpful with the BBC, with its international reputation, coming out and being so apparently hostile.

'We tried to build on BBC Sport's support and point out the differences with *Panorama*. I was very pleased with the way it went because it reinforced the commitment we had as a government and a country. For the IOC it was all about trusting the group of people presenting the bid and the Government showing it was right behind it.'

The London 2012 team also had another trick up its sleeve for winning friends.

The British Olympic Association had rented a villa close to the Olympic stadium to use for hospitality. Under the new strict bidding rules, Coe was not allowed to invite members to lavish receptions. But there was nothing wrong with Craig Reedie, an IOC member, asking other IOC members to join him at the BOA house, so an open invitation was handed out to all IOC members from the Scot. The villa, set in scenic grounds, was perfect for outdoor lunches and a dining area was set up around the swimming pool.

The idea was not to serve traditional British food. This villa was not there to serve tea, cakes or roast beef and Yorkshire pudding. The last image London 2012 wanted to portray was of Britain's old colonial past. A cook brought over from Britain was asked to use local produce to prepare a melange of international specialities. The message was: 'Forget that out-dated image of Britain. London has changed.'

A full programme of 'welcome events and lunches' was put into motion. IOC members interested in the bid could be taken upstairs to a marketing suite where a 3-D model of the Olympic Park in Stratford was set up and the walls were covered with both images of London and photographs or computerised images of the proposed 2012 venues. As another reminder that London's bid was being run by an Olympic gold medallist, photographs of Seb Coe's triumphs in Moscow and Los Angeles at the 1980 and 1984 Games were strategically placed along the walls.

'People were invited in small groups,' Lee explains. 'They could bring their spouses and kids if they wanted. It was a very relaxed atmosphere but we made sure the hospitality was not over the top. Members could pop by when they wanted but there was the occasional themed lunch. Cherie Blair and Tessa Jowell, for example, hosted an event to promote women in sport, which was attended by several key figures keen on increasing female participation.'

This entertaining essentially took place away from the TV cameras and newspaper reporters. It was important in building bridges with IOC members after the *Panorama* débâcle but it was given a real boost by the action and atmosphere unfolding in the sports stadiums of Athens.

Kelly Holmes had gone to the Olympics as a veteran middle-distance runner with a reputation for grabbing silver and bronze medals at major championships. But the 34-year-old former soldier, often hampered by injury, had struggled in the past to get everything right on the day and had missed out on winning gold on countless occasions. Although Kelly was well liked in both the British team and athletics press, none of them really expected that to change in Athens. Outside the world of athletics, Holmes was hardly known.

But the world was about to change dramatically for this shy woman from Kent on two brilliant nights in Athens, the second of which turned out to be a turning point for London's Olympic bid. For the first time in her career, Holmes was at the height of her physical fitness with no nagging injuries hampering her preparations. A late powerful surge down the home straight helped her just win the 800 metres title by the thickness of the designer dresses she was to wear at award ceremonies for the rest of the year. The look of astonishment on her face as she crossed the line will remain as one of the most memorable pictures in the history of British athletics.

Her 1,500 metres triumph was achieved less dramatically. But the historic double was part of an unforgettable last Saturday evening of the Games for Britain during which the men's sprint relay pulled off an historic defeat of the Americans to win the gold medal. Britain had enjoyed little success in the athletics and Holmes and the sprint relay boys had come to the rescue of a demoralised team. It was a poignant moment when Seb Coe presented Kelly with her gold medal.

Coe had been the Kent runner's hero when she was a child and the look on his face when he won the 1,500 metres in Moscow had been one of the most powerful memories of her childhood.

Usually when athletes – apart from those from the host nation – stand on the podium for their national anthems at Olympic Games, just a few spectators can be heard singing the words. But on that Saturday night in Athens, the Olympic stadium was covered with Union Jacks and the words of 'God Save the Queen' echoed around it. It was a perfect snapshot of Britain's passion for sport. IOC members had noticed that British fans made up, by far, the largest contingent of foreign fans in Athens. Despite all the worries about terrorism before the Games, sports fans from the UK had not been afraid to make the journey to Greece. Maybe it was because the British were used to jumping on cheap airline flights to Athens.

Whatever the background their presence in the stadiums was well received. Not only did they turn up for sports where Britain has a reputation for past success such as rowing and cycling, but they also made their way to the smaller sports at the Games where British competitors had little chance of winning. With their Union Jacks, they helped to create a superb atmosphere for the competitors.

All bidding cities talk about their country's passion for sport and IOC members are used to hearing it. But British fans were displaying their enthusiasm for the Olympics away from home. The IOC remembered the brilliant atmosphere at the 2000 Sydney Games when Australians embraced the event with all of their hearts. They were being given a taste of how Britain could match that Olympic fever if the Games came to London. The French, Spanish and even the Americans could not match this in Athens. Holmes, the relay squad and rowers, including Matthew Pinsent, who won a fourth gold medal and broke down in tears on the podium, showed how British competitors can be lifted to spectacular exploits by that kind of support.

Lee says: 'There were about twenty thousand fans in Athens and they made an impact in many of the venues. The medals won by Kelly, the sprint relay guys and by Matthew Pinsent were clinched by just a few centimetres but they were a very important part of helping the bid turn the corner in Athens. As a nation, we didn't just talk about our true passion for sport, we lived it. The success of our competitors was an important ingredient and so was the public support for the Games. IOC members had come to the Games with serious doubts about Britain and our commitment to Olympic sport. But they left it with the sound of celebrating British fans ringing in their ears. That was down to great characters like Kelly and Matthew and to the enthusiasm of the British sports fans. We felt very proud of them at the bid.

'I think our attitude surprised the other bids. They expected us to be in bad shape but, despite all of the difficulties, we got back on the front foot. During the Games, we had to make a presentation to the media of the London bid in the main press centre. We worked our socks off to get it right. It was Seb's debut before an international audience as bid leader and

London's first appearance before a global audience. But Seb, Ken Livingstone, Tessa Jowell and Steve Redgrave all delivered what neutrals described as the best presentation. We demonstrated that we were not put off by the rough waters we were sailing in.'

There is no doubt that Seb Coe was more exhausted at the end of the Athens Olympics than during any of his running days. But the efforts had been worth it. London was not completely clear of the fallout from the *Panorama* programme – there were serious concerns that the case could come back to haunt the bid since it was likely to be discussed in July 2005 in Singapore at the same meeting where the 2012 vote would be taken. Coe explains: 'There is no doubt that *Panorama* played into the hands of our enemies. They were saying: "The game is over for London. This is what you get now, imagine what it will be like if London gets the Games." But I never felt it was a deal-breaker although it was very serious.'

Lee adds: 'We felt we were back on track. We knew *Panorama* was still lurking in the background and still being exploited by our opponents. But in footballing terms, we had started 2–0 down and had brought the game back to 2–2 with the help of brilliant support from the GB team and fans. We needed that platform to move forwards to the next phase of the bid which was aimed at lifting public support for the campaign at home in time for IOC opinion polls later in the year. Athens was a make or break moment for London's bid and "Team Great Britain" worked together to save it.'

7. VISION ON THE MOUNT

On a cold but sunny day in mid-November 2004, Amber Charles, a talented fourteen-year-old basketball player from East Ham in the London borough of Newham handed in London's bid book to the International Olympic Committee at its headquarters on the banks of Lake Geneva. The 600-page document in English and French contained some of the most creative concepts ever put forward by a bidding city for a Summer Games: an athletes' village within a few minutes' walk of the main stadium; sport at some of the world's most famous venues – Wimbledon, Wembley, Horse Guards Parade and Hyde Park – and an Olympic Park that would change the face of London forever.

The bid book had successfully addressed the crucial issue of transport, one of the IOC's original criticisms of London's bid. It explained how high-speed trains on a new link from King's Cross station to Stratford in East London would carry hundreds of thousands of spectators to the Olympic Stadium in just seven minutes.

It was an impressive piece of work which had involved scores of people often working late into the night over a six month period. London's plans for the Games were split into key areas such as government and public support, the financing of the project, protection of the environment, transport, sports venues and the legacy for the city.

Britain had ticked all the boxes: Tony Blair was very much behind the bid; public support was increasing all the time; a realistic funding package had been put together mixing cash from the Lottery and London council tax payers and the compact Olympic Park meant the majority of athletes would compete within a short journey of their bedrooms.

The plans had already been praised in both the Olympic movement through the feedback from London's international presentations and in the domestic and foreign media. By allowing Amber Charles to hand in the documents to the IOC, London was showing that they wanted the 2012 Olympics to also be the Games for the next generation.

It was a special day for Amber who had been picked out to represent the children of East London. The IOC headquarters in Lausanne are situated in one of the most picturesque towns in mainland Europe. From the back of the building, IOC staff look down on a large park nestled beside Lake Geneva where they can go walking or jogging at lunchtime. On a clear winter's day, they have a spectacular view across the lake with snow-capped mountains in the distance. During the summer, they look out at an idyllic scene with boats crossing the lake and a park filled with mothers pushing prams, pensioners walking dogs and cyclists and joggers pumping clean Swiss air around their lungs.

East London was never going to have this kind of natural beauty on its doorstep. But part of London 2012's plans was to create the biggest new urban park in Europe for two hundred years in the Lee Valley, where families from less privileged backgrounds could enjoy similar activities outdoors. In addition to the new sports facilities, the Olympic Park would enhance the quality of life for East Londoners by creating a superb environment where they could get away from the bustle of city life. It was a wonderful dream to think that one of the most deprived areas of Britain, which was full of junk yards and scruffy streets, could be transformed into an idyllic city-living environment through the catalyst of an Olympic Park and the biggest sporting show on the planet. But anybody thinking on that November day that London 2012's bid book on its own was going to be enough to persuade the IOC to make it happen was incredibly naïve.

London 2012 had put together the best plans ever for an Olympics in Britain. But the view remained that London would lose a direct contest with Paris. The French had their main stadium in place; many IOC members would view Paris as a more attractive city; and the French capital also had the huge emotional pull that it had bid twice before for the Games and IOC members usually reward loyalty.

So, in November 2004, as Coe, Keith Mills and Craig Reedie prepared to travel around the world to speak to IOC members about London's bid, they and the team knew that they had to somehow find an extra ingredient in their bid that was powerful enough to lure IOC members away from the safe decision to vote for Paris.

Coe, Mills, Lee and marketing director David Magliano often sat in the bid offices at Canary Wharf talking about this issue. As experienced campaigners in local and national elections, Coe and Lee knew how important it was to find a message in the campaign that would strike a chord with the electorate. This was much harder than a traditional political election because the voters were such an eclectic group of people from countries of contrasting creeds and riches. This 'inner circle' was in a constant search for the final bid narrative, which could underpin the final push towards Singapore.

Coe was increasingly worried that today's children face a completely different range of distractions than he did in his childhood. From the late 1960s, when he had first watched the Olympics on a flickering black-and-white TV set, Coe had been inspired to take up running. In those days, kids could play football and cricket for hours in streets that were not full of speeding cars. It was the natural thing for children to play and follow football, cricket and athletics. Sitting indoors was not an option, especially at a time when daytime TV was in its infancy and computers were not household items. Coe had soon developed a passion for Chelsea Football Club, which in the late 1960s and early 1970s attracted fans from up and down the country because of its success. But Coe was worried that children are not inspired by sport in the same way that he was in his youth. In his view, young people of the 21st century appear to be fascinated by reality TV shows, with many seeking that kind of instant fifteen minutes of fame rather than an enduring place in history as a sporting champion.

An Olympics in London would definitely help address this issue. It would provide an inspiration for thousands of children in Britain to take up sport because the Games would dominate TV and the media. Role models like Paula Radcliffe and Kelly Holmes had already provided plenty of evidence of that. But Coe was not immediately sure how that concept could be used to help London win the Games.

It was clear that Olympic sports were not grabbing the attention of children in the early twenty-first century as they had in Coe's childhood. Coe explains, 'I remember my eleven-year-old daughter saying to me before the 2003 world athletics championships in Paris that only three kids in her class knew that the event was about to take place. At the same time she said to me that I didn't know who the skateboarder Tony Hawk was. If we had these issues in Britain then I was convinced that they also had them in Chicago, Paris and Tokyo.'

As the London campaign developed, the double Olympic champion sought advice from across the Olympic movement. One of the first people he approached after being appointed chairman in May 2004 was former International Olympic Committee President Juan Antonio Samaranch. Octogenarian Samaranch had been in charge of the IOC for 21 years after winning the Presidential election at the 1980 Moscow Olympics, the same Games where Coe produced his dramatic comeback after winning a disappointing silver in his favoured 800 metres to win the 1,500 metres title. Samaranch had always had a soft spot for Coe. Even during Coe's early running days, the Spaniard had recognised his obvious intelligence and his potential to be a serious sports administrator. It was a disappointment for the former IOC President that Coe first chose to go into British politics rather than follow a career in the IOC or in the IAAF, the governing body of athletics. Samaranch had not been alone in his opinion that Coe had a definite future in sports administration. Many senior figures in athletics saw the Olympic champion as a future President of the IAAF and were ready to campaign for him. Coe did sit on various IOC commissions but it was only in 2003 that he decided to return to high office in international sport and successfully campaigned for a place on the IAAF's council or cabinet.

When he stepped down from the presidency at the IOC Session in Moscow in the summer of 2001 and was replaced by Jacques Rogge, Samaranch had been very ill with kidney problems. It looked for some time that his days as an influential figure in the Olympic movement were over. But the Spaniard was a stubborn character who had run the IOC with a firm hand for two decades. He managed to bounce back to full fitness and engaged himself in his new role as the head of the Olympic Museum in Lausanne. At the same time, Samaranch was working hard for his son, Juan Antonio Samaranch junior, a successful financier, who had been appointed an IOC member towards the end of his father's presidency and was involved in Madrid's campaign. It was well-known in Olympic circles that Samaranch senior and junior had a lot of respect for Coe and London's campaign. While his first priority was supporting Madrid, it emerged that the former IOC President was prepared to say positive things to IOC members about London's bid. Coe's decision to fly to Barcelona for his advice would turn out to be crucial to the outcome of the 2012 campaign. As the vote got closer it became clear that Samaranch, now Honorary Life President of the IOC, was playing an active role in the race for the Games. And soon after the bid book went into IOC headquarters, one of Samaranch's most important former staff members also offered his advice to Coe.

Michael Payne is a former British champion in freestyle skiing who became the first serious marketing director of the IOC. Together with Canadian tax lawyer and IOC member, Dick Pound, Payne helped Samaranch set up a sponsorship programme, which revolutionised the finances of the IOC. When Samaranch became President, few cities were prepared to bid for the Games because mayors and Prime Ministers had seen the crippling tax burden they imposed on Montreal, the host of the 1976 Games. Pound and Payne set about drawing up a plan to attract blue-chip companies to become exclusive 'TOP' sponsors of the Games through multi-million dollar deals with the IOC. At the same time they started selling the

TV rights for the Winter and Summer Olympics in special packages. The TOP sponsors programme, which includes global companies like Coca-Cola, McDonald's, Kodak, Visa and Samsung, and the sale of the TV rights packages have since become an example of best practice for the sports marketing industry. The Olympics are the only major international sports event with no advertising boards in arenas. Yet the IOC has now managed to set up an exclusive club of sponsors who have special privileges in promoting their companies in host cities and have a high profile on TV broadcasts that carry advertisements between the action. The revenue from sponsors and TV has allowed the IOC to finance around 50 per cent of the running costs of most Olympic Games. That meant that the winning city of the 2012 campaign could expect to receive around £1 billion from the IOC.

As a marketing man, Payne has watched bidding cities come and go in numerous campaigns over two decades. He knows many IOC members personally and is well aware of what they had liked and disliked as far as the organisation of various Games was concerned. He is also a Londoner who was born in Swiss Cottage and went to school in the capital before moving abroad to compete on the ski circuit when he was eighteen.

The Athens Olympics had been Payne's last Games before he left the IOC to become marketing adviser to Bernie Ecclestone, owner and controller of Formula One motor racing. Therefore, from the autumn of 2004, Payne left his office and home in Lausanne and spent part of his week in Ecclestone's headquarters in central London. For the first few months, the former Olympic marketing guru was spending most of his time learning as much as he could about Formula One, but gradually he had time to turn his mind to London's bid. The American drawl in Payne's accent, acquired from hundreds of meetings with business leaders on the other side of the Atlantic, was gradually disappearing. He was starting to sound like a Londoner again and he was impressed by the capital's bid. He had been sceptical about London's chances of winning under Barbara Cassani because he feared members would be confused by an American running a British bid. But the marketing executive had been encouraging Coe to run a London bid for years and, once that became the case, he was prepared to offer his advice and become a sounding board for London 2012's plans.

Gradually, Coe was building interesting alliances in the Olympic and international sports movement and receiving top-class advice. An interesting jigsaw of powerful friends was being put together. Samaranch was not only an admirer of Coe but he was also a very good friend of Ecclestone, who brought his F1 show to the Spaniard's home town of Barcelona each year. The Formula One supremo is a Labour party supporter who has worked closely with Sports Minister Richard Caborn on issues such as the F1 track at Silverstone. Payne was an important link between them all. While he never took a penny from London 2012, the marketing expert emerged as one of the key advisers for London 2012's plans.

Payne left the IOC on the day after the closing ceremony of the Athens Olympics. A meeting with Richard Caborn, Payne and Ecclestone was arranged on the Formula One boss's spectacular yacht on a sunny day in the Greek port. Ecclestone's staff served chilled orange juice to the three men. There was important business to be discussed – the Sports Minister wanted to know what London had to do to win.

But it was not until snow had fallen on the mountains near his Swiss holiday home five months later that Payne and Coe linked up for a crucial chat. Payne invited Coe to his isolated chalet for a couple of days at the beginning of January 2005. On the edge of a forest, the restored farmhouse looks out on a glacier and a spectacular drop of 3,000 feet. Payne bought it because it enjoyed such an awe-inspiring view and he often goes there to think through important decisions in his life. Coe put on his snow shoes and he and Payne spent two days enjoying the fresh Alpine air. In the evening they would turn their minds to London's bid in the warmth of the chalet. Payne's chalet had already witnessed several crucial negotiations for Olympic TV deals. Now its wooden walls were listening to Coe talking about the ideas that he, Mike Lee and Keith Mills had been formulating in their top-floor headquarters in Canary Wharf.

Payne explains: 'I like the place because you can clear your head there and look at things in a different dimension. I could see the bid was getting serious and I thought Seb might need to step back from the details and really think through his vision and strategy. I just wanted to be a sounding board. London was always coming from behind. In a beauty contest it was not going to beat Paris, especially when you have a situation like a Stade de France already built versus a stadium in Stratford that does not exist. From a purely sports point of view, Paris had the advantage of bidding for a third time. It was clear that London had to offer something more. IOC members do understand the ability to change and can make historical decisions. If you give them options such as China for the 2008 Games or Seoul in 1988 they are capable of taking the Games to another level. Seb believed the whole youth problem fitted this remit. It was a real issue. In Olympic bidding what often matters is not what the Games can do for you and your city but what you can do for the Games. It is important not to sound arrogant but London was developing a very interesting vision.'

Payne was travelling the world on Formula One business but he remained just a phone call away as Coe, Lee, Mills and marketing expert David Magliano worked out how best to develop the vision of trying to use a London Games to inspire young people to take up sport. Wednesday nights at Canary Wharf became 'Presentation Nights'. From 6 p.m., Magliano and Lee would sit down with their teams in front of a TV and watch all the previous presentations by bidding cities to the IOC. It was painstaking work but London 2012 was looking for ways of putting over the developing vision to the IOC in a clear and compelling way.

Lee explains: 'The vision was worked on by Seb, Keith, David Magliano and myself. We bounced a lot of ideas off Craig Reedie and I would discuss a lot of the ideas with Jackie Brock-Doyle and Michael Pirrie from the communications team. We started developing the final narrative from six months out. When the Games had been in London before in 1948 and 1908, both London and the Games had been mutually enhanced. In 1948, for example, the Olympics saw the first volunteers programme which is a major part of the

Games today. So the question was: what could be special about London 2012?

'I felt that we needed the whole debate to move away from a discussion about five cities to a debate about a historical decision for the IOC about their future. The Olympic movement needed to take a leap with their 2012 decision. It needed to be bold but not risky. The 2012 race had to move into a vote that had historical implications for the IOC. That is what the 2008 decision had been all about – taking the Games to China for the first time. Michael Payne became part of a group of experts we used to bounce these ideas off. They were brainstorming sessions. We kept very quiet about them and they were very low key. The first one took place at a club in Knightsbridge and we met our friendly experts periodically and exchanged ideas directly and by phone.

'As we progressed we began to develop a vision that would lead to the brief for the New Moon film production company to prepare a special video for our presentation in Singapore. The idea was to show how Olympic champions are produced from a pyramid structure: a broad base of millions of children enjoying sport, then thousands of athletes competing, two hundred national champions, eighty Olympians and then eight Olympic finalists and an Olympic champion at the top. Without the broad base, the Olympic champions could not be produced. We also wanted to show that London was special because of its global reach. It was a major media centre and it had a huge diversity of cultures. Millions of young people from all over the world come to live in the capital. The idea was that London was the perfect place to start inspiring young people again to take up sport.'

At the same time Sebastian Coe was testing these views on a variety of IOC members and coming to the conclusion that many of them shared his concerns. Lee adds: 'It was not just an emotional issue either. NBC, the American TV network that has the exclusive rights to the Games in the United States, was increasingly worried that its audience was getting older. This – the inspiration of youth – was an idea that we thought could not only appeal to IOC members but also to the broadcasters and sponsors because it related to their concerns and future markets. Our narrative was really taking shape and the key phase of the lobbying of IOC members was now under way.'

Lobbying is a misleading word as far as London's bid for the 2012 Olympics is concerned. It gives the impression of people hanging about hotel lobbies and bars grabbing the attention of IOC members on their way to meetings and conferences. The expression has a haphazard air about it. While other cities have attempted to run a campaign for the Olympics along those lines, there was nothing haphazard about London's campaign to persuade IOC members to vote for Britain. It was run like a military operation with several battles being fought on various fronts. The IOC is a multifaceted organisation with a unique membership of millionaires, royalty and former Olympians. Around 117 of them would have the right to vote on 6 July 2005. They all have different views and contrasting reasons for supporting certain cities in Olympic votes, so a one-stop solution or sales strategy doesn't work in an organisation like this. London 2012 needed to sell the capital in 117 different ways, all linked to why London would be best.

Some IOC members are influenced by what a bidding city can achieve for the sport they run. Others are turned on by the prospect of the IOC making an historical statement with its decisions. And some members simply want to go to a city that they and their spouses will enjoy. Many members will vote for a particular city because it has the support of a member whom they like and who has backed their ideas in the past. Others are looking for trade-offs – support for something they want, for example, backing in an election for a place on the IOC's ruling executive board – in return for their vote. Other members will vote one way in one host-city election to influence the following one. For example, it was hard for the Austrian city of Salzburg to gain support in the race for the 2010 Olympics in 2003 because many European members wanted to make sure a city from their continent did not win the Winter Games. They had their eyes on the 2012 race where they wanted to support a European city. It clearly did not help if the Winter Games immediately before had gone to Europe.

The IOC is therefore an immensely complex political organisation. It is the cryptic crossword of sporting organisations multiplied by a factor of ten. There are few people who can answer all the clues. Plenty have attempted to simplify the workings of the IOC over the years and ended up falling on their faces like non-skaters on treacherous ice. There were also several who predicted a Paris victory more than a year before the 2012 vote and told London they were wasting their time by bidding. By doing so all these so-called experts did was show how little they knew about the organisation. Twelve months before Singapore, few IOC members had even thought about what they were going to do in the 2012 vote. So predicting the outcome so far away from the vote was a totally theoretical exercise.

The motto of Olympic bidding is clear: 'Fail to prepare and prepare to fail.' Approach a campaign with a one-dimensional strategy and failure is almost certain. The cities that have flopped in Olympic bidding races have usually been unable to understand the complexities of the membership. In the end they have looked like forelorn figures, completely lost in the IOC jungle without a map. The reason Juan Antonio Samaranch controlled the body so well for twenty years was that he could play this multidimensional chess. He could look three steps ahead in different directions and predict how he could gain support across the membership for what he wanted to do.

The other unwritten rule that a bidding city must understand is never to ask an IOC member: 'Can we count on your support?' IOC members guard their votes fiercely in a secret ballot. Almost none of them will say which way he or she plans to vote in public or in private. So it's an embarrassing question that IOC members will often refuse to answer. Bidding cities therefore have to identify members who have given enough hints that they are on their side in order to predict the number of votes they may receive. Despite their painstaking efforts to work out the numbers, most bidding cities get it wrong. The history of Olympic bidding is full of cities saying they are confident of getting fifty votes and ending up with just fifteen. The 2012 race was to be no different.

Michael Payne explains: 'The most important thing is to understand the membership. You have to find out what they want in the future. Status is important for them. Many do like the pageantry of the setting of an Olympic Games. They are looking for a bidding city that can provide the pixie dust. But a broad brushstroke approach doesn't work. You have to profile all the individuals and understand them. For the IOC, giving the Olympics to a city is like handing over your baby to a school. You have to be able to trust the school with your child and be confident that they will nurture it.

'Basically, bidding is about becoming everybody's best friend and winning their trust. So you have to approach the whole thing like a military campaign with discipline and a game plan. Nothing can happen by chance. You have to know what you are going to say to IOC members and when and who is going to deliver the message. Some care about the athletes just involved in their sport. Others have a bigger political vision. And in the 2012 campaign, you were not necessarily campaigning for first-round votes. This campaign was always going to be so close that it would need four rounds of voting before one city got a majority. So one member might vote completely differently in each round.'

London 2012 attacked the lobbying from several different angles with Seb Coe, Keith Mills, Craig Reedie, Debbie Jevans, the sports director, and Tessa Jowell and Richard Caborn from the government all actively involved in the campaign.

It was important that IOC members saw Sebastian Coe as the leader of the bid and the main carrier of London's message. As a double Olympic champion, he was the most recognisable sporting figure in the whole of the 2012 campaign, for both the IOC and the media. He had also built up contacts through the IOC from his days on the track. In the last six months of the campaign, Coe travelled the world to conferences of both the IOC and national Olympic committees as well as to major sport events, which were often attended by IOC members.

Keith Mills was Coe's right-hand man. Although he was unknown in the IOC at the start of the bid, the London 2012 chief executive was to build up huge respect in the Olympic movement by 6 July 2005. This is a man who, until he took up the job of chief executive of London 2012, was also hardly known by the general public. His ideas have been influencing the lives of millions of Britons for decades, however.

In his mid-fifties, Mills is the son of a Brentwood ball-bearings factory worker who was brought up in a council house and left school at fifteen to start a menial job in Fleet Street. He first started to work in marketing at *The Economist* and at the *Financial Times* before striking out on his own to set up a dozen companies and becoming a multi-millionaire. He is best known for inventing customer-loyalty schemes. He dreamed up the concept of Air Miles on a train from Liverpool to London and sold the idea to British Airways in 1987. Now he runs the company behind Nectar cards, the biggest customer-loyalty scheme in Britain. It is worth an estimated £250 million.

But Mills is not a man who flashes his money around. Although he is always immaculately dressed and drives a Bentley, he is an extremely modest man who is never surrounded by scores of assistants, like some millionaires. He has strong links with sport and is a keen amateur sailor who was part of the crew that won the famous Clipper yacht race in 1998. He also set up a racing company, which backed Alex Thomson's 2004 Vendée Globe campaign, the non-stop single-handed round-the-world race.

IOC members like to mix with powerful business figures and Mills fitted the bill perfectly. His love of sailing, the Olympic event of IOC President Jacques Rogge and other key Olympic figures, meant he could also talk passionately about sport.

But his greatest quality for London 2012 was as a calm listener. Maybe it came from his experience in building new businesses but Mills did not run around the world trying to deliver a hard sell to IOC members. He listened carefully to their ideas and calmly turned them into London 2012 lobbying policy. Even during difficult days for the bid, he remained calm and composed. He was the perfect lobbying partner for Coe.

Craig Reedie explains: 'Keith is simply the nicest of men, a super bloke. The international sports world likes the presence of substantial businessmen. He was both knowledgeable about business and a successful marketing man. Many members said to me what a nice man he was and he became very popular. The most important thing was that in the middle of all the frantic efforts to win the bid, he remained so calm. That was a real plus to the bid.'

Reedie, himself, was also one of the most important players in the lobbying game. Unlike Coe and Mills, the 64-year-old Scot had the unrestricted right to talk to as many of his fellow IOC members as he liked and wherever he liked. Given that Britain's other IOC member, the Princess Royal, was unable to work on the bid intensely because of her busy diary, the responsibility fell to Reedie to play the 'libero' role and jet around the world to work on his friendships within the movement. A former financier who played international badminton in the 1960s, Reedie has been an IOC member since 1994 and has forged alliances across the movement through his work on various commissions. He has been a member of the IOC's marketing commission for a decade and sits on the council of the World Anti-Doping Agency (WADA), the body responsible for international anti-doping activity. He also sat on the evaluation commission for the 2008 bidding race won by Beijing and is therefore an expert at looking at bidding campaigns from the IOC's side.

As chairman of the British Olympic Association, he also represented the IOC in Britain. London knew that it was important that the BOA was seen by IOC members to be a central part of the bid. The message to members had to be that this was a campaign run by sport, not by politicians. When Tony Blair met members in one-on-one meetings later in the campaign, Reedie was there to introduce them to the Prime Minister. Reedie explains: 'When Manchester and Birmingham did their bids, the BOA always danced to the bid team's tune and we got nowhere. This time we had to have a central role. Every time London made a presentation, I started it. I also made use of the international travel I was allowed to do for WADA and the commissions. I never missed a meeting of those commissions. I would stop off on the way back from trips and play golf with an IOC member or have lunch. Having been a member since 1994, I knew quite a few members pretty well.'

Coe, Mills and Reedie were the three front-line figures of the lobbying campaign. Their main job was to build up trust among IOC members and convince them that Britain was serious about hosting the Games this time. This was not done by intensive briefings about London's plans for the Games. It was achieved by listening to IOC members and responding to their concerns. Mills's job, as the least well-known figure in the IOC, was not to preach but to show that London was well aware of the needs of international sport and was prepared to find solutions to problems. This could range from providing an excellent arena or environment for a sport in London to helping with international marketing efforts. Coe talked about his concerns about young people taking up sport and listened to the views of IOC members on the subject. Reedie, meanwhile, sought out his friends in the Olympic movement and worked on engaging their support for London through friendship. None of the three ever bluntly asked a member how they would vote. What mattered was trust and confidence in London. In short, London 2012 wanted to show it was a 'listening bid which cared about sport and the Olympic movement'. Perception is the key to everything in the IOC. If key people in the IOC started talking about London in a positive way, it had a snowball effect.

Michael Payne explains: 'One of the most important things is to get members to debate your issues and talk about your bid amongst themselves. You have to talk about issues that they care about. What members say to other members is important. All Juan Antonio Samaranch would have to say to members, for example, is that "the British are serious this time" and that would add huge credibility.'

Coe, Mills and Reedie spent little time in Britain in the final six months of the bid. Their schedules included high-profile Olympic meetings and presentations in Brisbane, Ghana and Berlin. Their campaigning was mostly visible. But other key figures were also working quietly in the background on what is known as the 'secret war'.

The detailed planning and coordinating of the lobbying, for example, was drawn up by Andrew Craig, a former colleague of Payne who helped set up the IOC's successful TOP sponsorship programme and worked on Vancouver's triumphant bid for the 2010 Winter Games. Craig was born in Britain but he lives in Detroit where he used to be involved in the marketing of the Cart motor sports series.

Britain had to lift the profile of London's bid across the world. Although Foreign Secretary Jack Straw was not a front-line member of the lobbying team, the Foreign Office played an important role in helping Andrew Craig in the planning. London 2012 officials were not allowed to approach IOC members directly in their own countries, but it was important that foreign governments and sporting authorities were aware of London's campaign. Working closely with bid political relations expert, John Zerafa, Craig would ask the Foreign Office for advice on improving contacts across the globe. In many countries British ambassadors have huge respect and work was done to ensure ambassadors saying the right thing to an influential sports figure at a reception in Mexico City or Rio. IOC members were invited to functions that had nothing to do with London 2012 but generally improved relations between the member and Britain. Feedback was also given on political and media attitudes to London's bid around the world.

The government had done its homework on what role it could play in trying to win votes across the world. Lord Patrick Carter, the head of the Lottery distributor Sport England who was the best man at both weddings of Jack Straw, took a particular interest in the lobbying process in the early part of the bid. Although Carter was not a front-line lobbyist, his advice is well respected by senior figures in the government, including the Prime Minister, on a range of issues. Officially Carter was responsible for running the legacy aspects of the bid. But he was also very interested in how Britain could use all of its diplomatic influence in persuading IOC members to support London. He helped ensure that Jack Straw got engaged in the process.

Culture Secretary Tessa Jowell and Sports Minister Richard Caborn used every opportunity they could to promote the bid during routine international governmental meetings. Caborn was able to work on the votes of the Commonwealth through regular meetings of Commonwealth Sports Ministers. He had hosted the inaugural meeting of Commonwealth Sports Ministers at the 2002 Commonwealth Games in Manchester before the bid was launched. He organised another similar summit in

Athens just before the 2004 Olympics. There are no real blocs of votes in the IOC but London felt it could win over many Commonwealth members because of strong traditional ties with Britain, and London was the only city from the Commonwealth in the race.

The Sports Minister had particularly strong links with influential South African IOC member Sam Ramsamy, who had been exiled in London for twenty years during the apartheid regime. Caborn had worked closely with the anti-apartheid movement during that time and was a director of two major pop concerts at Wembley in support of Nelson Mandela. Caborn went to South Africa during the bidding campaign to persuade former South African President Mandela to publicly back the bid. His pledge of support was to be used in London's final presentation to the IOC in Singapore.

Caborn was also involved in helping the World Anti-Doping Agency to win the support of governments worldwide in their battle against the abuse of performance-enhancing drugs in sport. Attending WADA meetings was immensely helpful to the bid because the organisation included eighteen IOC members. For the first time for several years, Britain was seen as a key player in trying to solve important issues in sport. Caborn built up a particularly good relationship with WADA Chief Dick Pound.

Caborn explains: 'It was important that Britain was seen to play a proactive role in helping things like the WADA code against drugs to be implemented. Britain had not been punching its weight internationally before.'

Caborn's links with Formula One's Bernie Ecclestone and his close relationship with football's Premier League Chairman Dave Richards were also important. Both men travelled the world and regularly met influential sports figures. They helped build the perception about London 2012's professionalism. 'Bernie was important because he had such great contacts and he spoke regularly to influential people in the sports world. He lobbied for us,' says Caborn. 'The Premier League is also very powerful globally with three-quarters of a billion people watching it every weekend. All the clubs supported us and Dave Richards used his international contacts to promote the bid.

'The British Council had also set up a link between schools in Britain and schools abroad called "Dreams and Teams". It involved exchanges between young people around sport. The Foreign Office was really tuned into this. It involved a lot of countries in Eastern Europe and Africa. The embassies put together sporting evenings. There was nothing against the rules in this.'

Through Britain's presidency of the European Union during the latter part of the bid, Tessa Jowell regularly came into contact with senior ministers, some of whom were involved in the Olympics. Mario Pescante, the Italian Sports Minister, who is also an influential IOC member, was a classic example. Jowell and Caborn had every right to talk to the Italian Sports Minister and Pescante was in many ways a litmus test for London's campaign. As a former campaign manager for Jacques Rogge when he was running for the IOC presidency, he was one of the most powerful IOC members in Europe. Caborn, for example, had the opportunity to speak to Pescante and his Italian IOC colleague Franco Carraro in Istanbul at the European Cup final in May 2005 between Liverpool and AC Milan. Jowell would also regularly run into IOC members, who were involved in government business. As a Cabinet minister who is a close political ally of Tony Blair, Jowell's job was to explain the passion of both the Prime Minister and the government for London's bid.

None of these informal and formal meetings broke the IOC rules since they were taking place for reasons other than the 2012 campaign. But they were important in boosting the perception in the IOC that the government was firmly behind the bid.

Andrew Craig also recruited officials to concentrate on particular regions of the world, providing feedback about London's progress as well as advising on how best to influence IOC members. John Boulter, a French speaker in his mid-sixties, was responsible for Africa and the French-speaking world. Boulter, a former Olympic 800-metre runner, has an Olympic contacts book to die for after a long career working internationally for the shoe and sportswear company Adidas. The German-based company has often been closely linked with both the IOC and FIFA, the world governing body of football. While London regarded the Commonwealth as 'its territory', Paris had good reason to see Africa's French-speaking countries as their home ground. But London was doing its best to turn it into part of London's territory and Boulter was a key player in that. Many Olympic officials in Africa remembered Boulter as a man who had been helpful to them in the past. The former Adidas executive also had good contacts with key figures in the international sports federations, several of whom had been involved with Adidas over the years.

London also recruited the Canada-based former journalist Carlos Garcia, who originally hailed from Uruguay and was a formidable networker in the Olympic world of Central and South America. He had also worked on Vancouver's bid for the 2010 Games and was a respected figure in Olympic circles.

Another key area was the international sports federations. Increasingly, the Presidents of key sports federations were being appointed as IOC members. London was keen to show the international sports world that it regarded the international federations as key players in the Games. While the IOC takes responsibility for the overall staging of the Games, the organisation of the actual sports events at the Olympics is the responsibility of the federations. They set the rules, arrange the layout of the venues and bring in the officials to stage the events. In many ways, they are the most important clients of a Games organising committee together with the athletes. So, when London 2012 was appointing a sports director, it chose a woman who knew this world like the back of her hand.

Debbie Jevans is a former junior Wimbledon champion who went on to become general secretary of the International Tennis Federation. Having been responsible for the tennis competition at previous Olympics, she had sat through many meetings of organising committees and international federations. She knew the complaints sports usually had about Olympic organising committees. Most federations wanted to be able to stage 'test events' at Olympic venues in the year before the Games, for example. They also needed to get their officials into countries well in advance to help organisers work on the layout of venues. The international sports world needed to trust London to be a solid partner if Britain won the Games. Jevans knew how London could impress this crucial group of officials. As one of the few women in a high position in an international federation, she has a reputation of being an intelligent administrator and is well liked.

Information was the most important commodity in the whole of this campaign. With the help of Craig Reedie and Andrew Craig's team of advisors, London was building up a picture of every IOC member and their views on key Olympic issues. This meant that every time anybody from London 2012 came into contact with an IOC member, they were aware of important background information.

However short a conversation was, Coe, Mills, Reedie or Jowell knew what to say and, as importantly, what not to say to IOC members. This information was later to be given to Tony Blair before he met IOC members in one-on-one meetings. The lobbying team was also constantly providing information on political issues within the IOC, which could have an impact on the bid. London 2012 was managing to play the three-dimensional chess needed to win, thinking several moves ahead and being aware of the possible obstacles standing in their way.

Mills explains: 'There are two phases of lobbying. The first is information gathering and the other is using the information. We spent 23 months working on phase one and then first started using phase two in the final month. Right at the start of the bid I invited John Furling over from Vancouver. He had run Canada's successful bid for the 2010 Winter Games. He spent the whole campaign spending as much time as possible with IOC members. We learned that it is important to talk to IOC members and ask their views about things like sport in their country and what they liked about the successful Sydney Games, for example. They all have different profiles and relationships are important. People don't vote for people they don't like just as people don't do business with people they don't like. We knew that each city had core supporters and they would never change. We basically ring-fenced them. But everybody else was up for grabs. We built up profiles on each member. These were basically reports on conversations we had

had with members. Then we targeted sports events and conferences. I filled up two passports with stamps and visas travelling around the world. I must have spent around three quarters of the year on the road in the last year of the campaign. The travel budget was about £2 million. But we had one million pounds worth of free flights from BA and Virgin Atlantic to help us. Seb and I drew up a list of members who we would work on. It made sense, for example, for me to talk to business people in the IOC while Seb talked to athletes. What is important is that you have got to listen more than you talk. I was once told that the best salesmen are people who keep quiet and make sure the conversation revolves around the client and not you.'

The bid therefore fought the 2012 lobbying campaign on six key fronts:

1. The influencing of IOC members through presentations at Olympic meetings and the communications campaign.
2. The one-on-one chats around the world with IOC members involving Craig Reedie, Sebastian Coe and Keith Mills.
3. The Foreign Office-aided promotion of London's sporting concept through subtle diplomacy.
4. The hunt for support from the international world of both sport and politics through political channels involving Tessa Jowell and Richard Caborn.
5. The targeting of key regions in the world using the expertise of John Boulter and Carlos Garcia.
6. The lobbying of international sports federation Presidents through the expertise of Debbie Jevans.

All this lobbying work was being done alongside the crucial communications campaign where London's plans and ideas were reaching IOC members through the international media, where London was generating twice as much coverage as all the other bid cities combined. And from November 2004, London could step up the international campaign and promote the bid outside Britain. It was a joined-up, integrated and targeted approach, which was to leave their rivals in their wake.

London spread their message through their increasingly effective international presentations, head-to-head with the other bids, and well-received media initiatives. Together with the lobbying campaign this all served to improve gradually Britain's image around the world as a potential host for the Games. IOC members needed to be confident that they could hand over the Olympics and trust Britain to look after them; they needed to know that the British government was serious about supporting this bid; they needed to be sure that Sebastian Coe and Keith Mills really understood the needs of both the IOC and international sports federations. Slowly but surely, London's creative vision for London 2012 was starting to persuade IOC members that there was an historic dimension to the Singapore vote.

This work with the voters was vital but it rarely made headlines. It was a largely underground 'secret war' and London was certainly winning a few battles over the French who were also working the world through their IOC members and their diplomatic channels.

In the media, the 2012 debate often raged around issues that did not have a significant impact on the bid. At the start of 2005, for example, British newspapers were full of reports that the Queen had undermined the campaign by backing Paris to win the vote. In a private conversation during a reception at Buckingham Palace, the Queen was reported to have told an East End teenager she was worried Londoners were not fully behind the bid. At the same time there were also suggestions that Prince Harry's controversial decision to wear a Nazi uniform to a friend's party was also damaging to the bid. Although these two stories sparked much interest around the world, the bid team were relaxed. Their focus was on the voters, the pro-bid messages they were receiving and on the 'secret war' where the quiet conversations were convincing the team that winning was becoming a real possibility.

8. MORE POLISH THAN THE FRENCH

May is a beautiful month in Paris. The colours of spring fill the city's parks and gardens and the sun shines down on thousands of tourist couples seeking to rekindle the romance in their relationships with a stroll through the beautiful Jardin des Tuileries to the Louvre.

In May 2005, Parisians had an extra spring in their step. There was a real belief in France that by the time the summer came along the capital would win the right to stage the 2012 Olympics. IOC inspectors had visited all the bidding cities in February and March and the International Olympic Committee was about to publish the report from its evaluation commission on the five cities entering the vote on 6 July. It was an open secret that Paris would receive the best rating and Olympic experts and bookmakers were confidently predicting a Paris victory. The French capital was already starting to party.

The attention of the world's media always turns to the French capital in May and early June when the French Open tennis tournament is staged at the city's scenic Roland Garros complex, one of the city's proposed Olympic venues. The clay-court tournament, the second grand slam of the year held a few weeks before the players head to Wimbledon, is a magnet for millionaires, movies stars and models, whose appearances at courtside in designer sunglasses and the latest fashions grab the attention of photographers and the TV cameras. The image is sent around the world that Paris is the chic place to be in spring. In 2005, the French were preparing for a special Olympic festival on the Champs Élysées on the same day as the men's tennis final at Roland Garros. It was perfect timing, just 24 hours before the publication of the evaluation commission report.

More than a million people were set to turn up on France's most famous avenue, transformed for the day into a sporting playground with a swimming pool, running track and wrestling mats. It was a clever public relations coup. Spectacular pictures of Parisians gathering on the Champs Élysées to play sport would be published around the world just as the IOC was about to hand the city a glowing report. The message about France's passion for the Games would reach IOC members everywhere. The city was looking and acting like a winner.

This was one of the high points of the Paris 2012 campaign. Philippe Baudillon, the chief executive of the bid, should have been enjoying the Parisian sunshine and calmly looking forward to the celebrations. But the former diplomat was far from happy. In a phone call to Seb Coe he requested that his London counterpart act to curb London's communications campaign and in particular the role of director, Mike Lee. Baudillon claimed Lee's behaviour was not acceptable under the International Olympic Committee's ethics rules which ban bidding cities from criticising each other in public.

Coe, clearly astonished that the head of the Paris bid would make such a claim, tried to assuage a man whom he had learned to respect greatly during the 2012 battle. But the double Olympic champion was certainly not going to reprimand his chief strategist as London entered the decisive stage of the bidding race. He was also not going to take any criticism from his main rival. Lee has a reputation among journalists for being a tough spin doctor who can be demanding and aggressive at times. But Coe knew that he had not been personally targeting the chief executive of the Paris bid.

What the incident did show, however, was that London's steady progress in the 2012 race during the six months since the bid books were handed into the IOC appeared to be rattling Paris. London was dominating the international media campaign and huge gains were being made through the sophisticated lobbying by Seb Coe, Keith Mills, Craig Reedie and the government.

The evaluation commission's visit to Britain in February 2005 had also been a huge success and, from the work of the lobbying team, it was becoming clear that the bid was becoming very popular among key figures in the international sports federations.

London looked by far the most creative of the five bids at a crucial stage of lobbying and international promotion. In short, London 2012 was catching up the French favourites fast and its campaign was gathering momentum with every passing day. Like a front-runner hearing and feeling the breath of a challenging athlete behind, Paris appeared to be getting nervous.

Lee explains: 'We interpreted the Baudillon incident as an interesting sign of panic in the Paris team. The suggestion that I was briefing against them showed that the French were clearly rattled by our communications campaign. We ran a more aggressive campaign than Paris but we had to. We were coming from behind and if you want to win a race from behind, it's no good running at the same pace as the leader. We had to develop momentum and continually develop stories and the bid's narrative. The British media demanded that of us and in that sense they made us a better communications team.

'Britain is simply a more challenging environment in which to work. Looking back, it was clear that, while we had strong leadership, it seemed that Baudillon was being increasingly sidelined by the politicians in France. That was no secret. Any journalist who went to the evaluation commission visit to Paris in the previous March could see that all the politicians at national, regional and city level wanted to have their say. The mayor of Paris, Bertrand Delanoe, acted as the official head of the bid and was also determined to stamp his mark on the campaign. Winning the Games would have enhanced his reputation greatly and could potentially have given him a shot at the French presidency.

'Seb Coe did not have these political problems. Of course, Tessa Jowell and Ken Livingstone wanted to put over their particular aims for the bid but they always fitted their comments into the general narrative or message. Nobody was trying to upstage anybody else. We all worked as a team. The French did not appear to have the same teamwork.'

Certainly Delanoe was a confident and eloquent speaker and he appeared to be someone who loved the spotlight. It was nevertheless a tactical mistake by Paris not to use Baudillon's skills more in public. One year from his fiftieth birthday, he was by far the most talented linguist on the Paris bid. He spoke almost faultless English and, in interviews with the media, he rarely put a foot wrong in terms of the statements he made. A graduate of ENA (École Nationale d'Administration), France's top business school where Presidents Valéry Giscard d'Estaing and Jacques Chirac were educated, Baudillon spent much of his career living abroad as a diplomat and then as a TV executive. He specialised in Middle East and African affairs and for a time served at the United Nations in New York. While a former advisor to the French government, Baudillon also came to the Paris bid with plenty of experience in the world of sport. He was involved in the planning and construction of the Stade de France, the Paris stadium built for the 1998 football World Cup, which will also play host to the 2007 rugby World Cup and was the centrepiece of the French capital's bid. Crucially, he also took part in the failed Paris bid for the 1992 Olympics and had a detailed knowledge of why the French had lost to Barcelona in that campaign.

Few of Paris's rivals were fooled by the three-day stubble which sometimes decorated the Frenchman's chin: Baudillon was a good operator who had made many friends in the Olympic movement.

Part of the chief executive's problem, however, was that his speeches did not come across as being very passionate. In many ways he is extremely 'un-French' in that respect, though he is a far better communicator in English than Delanoe.

In Olympic bidding, it is also very important that the person who has made all the friends in the IOC is seen to be a key figure in the organisation. By sidelining Baudillon, the French were weakening the trust between the bid and the members. The other factor was that members also tend to show more faith in bid leaders than politicians. This is simply because politicians can easily disappear from office after elections whereas bid leaders are more likely to have a duty to remain for seven years to follow the project through.

Jon Tibbs, the Briton running the international media campaign for Paris, believes the French made a mistake over Baudillon. He says: 'Increasingly it appeared that Philippe was unable to front up major presentations and initiatives. That almost became the exclusive domain of the mayor and the Minister of Sport, Jean-François Lamour. There were times when it almost seemed that they were competing to take the lead at any given event. That was a great shame. Seb Coe was being praised as a leader and growing in stature while Philippe as a leader seemed to be increasingly marginalised.'

The 'politicising' of the Paris bid was clear for the international media to see in March 2005 when each senior politician took his turn to add their answer to the same question during the visit by the evaluation commission. Some 'Olympic beat' journalists were starting to ask themselves how an organising committee would be able to operate if everything had to be agreed by a committee of politicians with different agendas. But these concerns did not stop Paris from holding on to its position as firm favourite in the race with a glowing evaluation commission report providing a further boost.

The commission's job is to visit all the candidate cities and write a detailed report on their ability to stage the Games, focusing on key areas like transport, finance, sports venue construction, the environment and political and public support. The report, which is sent to IOC members one month before the vote, is important but not decisive.

The reality is that internal politics and dynamics in the IOC play as big a role as technical factors in Olympic votes. Only a few IOC members actually read the findings in detail and most will dip in and out of the technical report to read about a particular aspect of the Games which interests them. Nevertheless bidding cities have to attach a huge amount of importance to the visit of the evaluation commission because they know that, while the city with the best report may not win, a bad showing can be extremely damaging.

When the commission went to Paris in early spring, the French pulled out all the stops. Paris packaged five million baguettes in special 2012 wrappers, the Eiffel Tower was dressed up with a huge bid sign and there was even an Olympic billboard at the Louis Vuitton fashion store on the Champs Élysées. It was a clever marketing ploy. All of France's famous products were backing the bid. Each of the inspectors' rooms at the luxurious Grand Hotel was carefully chosen to make sure it had a perfect view over the Opéra Square. A vase of fresh flowers, a bowl of fruit and a plate of special macaroons was slipped on to the table next to the sofa in every room each day. Style was important. And so was romance. '*L'amour des Jeux aux coeurs de nos vies*' ('Love of the Games at the heart of our lives') shouted the slogan from the fancy decorations around France's famous bread and bijoux.

'*L'amour des grèves*' – France's love of strikes – was dominating the media in March 2005, however. There had been concerns that tens of thousands of French workers marching in the city to protest against labour reforms and air and train strikes during the week would mar the visit. The media highlighted the disruption but the evaluation commission inspectors, a mixture of IOC members and experts in Olympic planning, were whisked around in buses surrounded by police outriders. The motorcyclists made sure the roads were cleared of traffic and the inspectors made their way around the city in record time. Interestingly, London and Madrid had been told by the IOC not to use outriders for visits to venues but the French got away with it.

Even the news that France's IOC member and former Sports Minister Guy Drut was facing charges of corruption failed to stop the commission leaving the city feeling very positive about the Paris bid. Technically, the French were perceived to have an extremely strong bid. Their main stadium, the Stade de France, had struggled with viewing problems for spectators at the 2003 World Athletics Championships but, in general, it was seen as a huge advantage to be able to take the inspectors to a finished stadium rather than a proposed building site. The Paris plans were also impressive with beach volleyball scheduled for a spectacular setting in front of the Eiffel Tower and plans for certain events to be held at the magnificent Versailles Palace. The city's legacy argument was nowhere near as strong as that of London's – the Games would not change Paris in the same way they could transform East London – but the French capital was perceived as a very safe bet. After the problematic build-up to the 2004 Athens Games, that was seen as a sound reason for the IOC to give the Games to the city.

Although Baudillon refused to admit in public that Paris was the favourite, it was clear that the French had every reason to be quietly confident about the commission's report due in June.

London, however, had also enjoyed a successful visit from the evaluation commission back in February. It had required painstaking planning by the bid team and, before the commission members even set foot on British soil, every detail of every venue site visit and presentation was rehearsed several times.

The thirteen-member team, which visited London for four days, was headed by Moroccan Nawal El Moutawakel, the first woman from an Islamic nation to win an Olympic medal when she took gold in the 400 metres hurdles at the 1984 Los Angeles Games. She was a fluent English speaker and knew Seb Coe well from their shared sporting and charity interests. The commission also included Sam Ramsamy, South Africa's IOC member and anti-apartheid campaigner, and Namibian sprinter Frank Fredericks who had strong links with several British athletes. The IOC's executive director Gilbert Felli headed the administrative staff. Apart from one final press conference, the commission members were kept away from the media. This was usual practice for such visits because it was important that they did not pass immediate comment on what they had seen.

The commissioners were left in no doubt, however, even when they arrived, that London was dressing up for their benefit. The Olympic officials were given a VIP welcome when they arrived on separate planes from various parts of the globe. 'Back the Bid' banners were hung at airports and along the route to the Four Seasons Hotel near Canary Wharf where the commissioners were based.

The visit began in difficult circumstances. Ken Livingstone was making headlines at home and abroad because he had compared a Jewish reporter Oliver Finegold from London's *Evening Standard* to a 'concentration-camp guard'. The comments were made after the reporter asked Livingstone questions following a reception to celebrate the twentieth anniversary of former MP Chris Smith coming out as gay. The *Evening Standard* chose not to publicise the incident at first, saying reporters were often confronted with abuse and that it was part of the rough and tumble of news gathering. But details of the incident broke on another paper's website and the story began to dominate the news agenda at the start of the visit. This was a problem, given that many international reporters had come to London to cover the visit and the story grew, threatening to overshadow the commission's visit. Tony Blair, among others, called on Livingstone to apologise but the mayor refused.

Lee says: 'The whole thing was causing us concern and we made various representations to Ken and his advisers, and arranged for Seb and Ken to have a private meeting. If this had happened at another time, it would have been less of an issue but there was potential damage on the eve of the evaluation commission's visit. We were not looking for an apology directly to the journalist because we knew Ken was not prepared to do that. We were looking more for an apology to people who might have been offended. It was clear, however, that Ken had very firm views linked to a broader principle about never apologising under media pressure and letting the media control the agenda. We knew the controversy was being reported internationally and that it would come up at a special press conference for the international media with myself, Ken and Tessa Jowell on the eve of the visit. It didn't take long for Alan Abrahamson of the *Los Angeles Times* to ask the question.

'Ken made it clear that it was a separate issue to the London bid and I reinforced that point. I think that strategy worked because there were enough experienced Olympic journalists about who knew that these kinds of domestic controversies come and go and that the IOC is a sophisticated global organisation. We were also about to go into a busy media period with two press conferences each day and I was hopeful that the whole thing would dissolve.'

Livingstone was adamant that he was not going to give in to media pressure. The Mayor explains: 'I have had twenty-five years of dealing with the British media and the minute they ramp up the pressure on me to change a policy or something I say: "The day I give in, my usefulness to London finishes because they will know my breaking point." It's the straightforward law of them wanting power without responsibility and you can't give in to it. In that sense this was a relatively trivial thing compared to the pressure that was brought to bear about not doing the congestion charge, which was pretty overwhelming, and I didn't get elected to do what the British media want. They can go and boil their heads collectively. What I picked up on by Athens was that these IOC members were not terribly interested in party politics. These are people whose whole lives have been focused on sport or business and I think they largely can see that the history of political involvement in the Games has been damaging, a succession of boycotts and so on. They just want a marvellous Games and to make sure nothing gets in the way of that.'

The commission began their London visit with a nine-hour day of detailed presentations on key themes including transport, security, the environment and funding. In addition to Seb Coe and his London 2012 officials, they were addressed by Culture Secretary Tessa Jowell, environmental campaigner Jonathan Porritt and Sir Ian Blair, Commissioner of the Metropolitan Police. Double Olympic champion Kelly Holmes was one of the well-known Olympians to appear before the commission along with triple jumper Jonathan Edwards and Olympic champions, Daley Thompson and Sir Steve Redgrave. Holmes told the Olympic inspectors that London would stage an Olympics with more 'buzz and atmosphere' than any other Games because of Britain's passion for sport. A key role was also played by multi-gold medallist Paralympian, Tanni Grey-Thompson, and British Paralympic Association Chairman, Mike Brace, who reinforced the message of London's commitment to the Paralympics.

London 2012 arranged for the production company Live to set up a special presentation room in the Four Seasons Hotel.

It contained a large three-dimensional model of the proposed Olympic Park. Lee explains: 'Quite a lot of the visit involved hotel-based presentations so we created an interesting environment where we could use video, models and images to bring alive the proposed venues. We had a first rehearsal of the visit two weeks before the inspectors arrived where I acted as the Commission chairman. The final dress rehearsal was with Craig Reedie in that role so we could use his experience as a member of the Commission which visited the cities bidding for the 2008 Games, which included Paris. This dress rehearsal was crucial – we brought in several outside experts and Craig put us through our paces.

Although the whole schedule had been agreed with the IOC, we knew from the earlier visit to Madrid that it was possible that they would ask to change the schedule to see how we would react. We had contingency plans in place in case any member suddenly asked to visit one of the venues outside of London, such as the sailing venue in Weymouth. We also had plans in place to provide emergency medical care if one of the commissioners took ill. We thought of every possible scenario. It was important to show that we could think on our feet because that is exactly what is often needed in the middle of an Olympic Games if a problem arises. The preparation team did a fantastic job.'

The following day the inspectors completed a whirlwind tour of the key venues with Seb Coe as the main tour guide. The commission was divided into three parties and taken around the proposed venues, focusing on the main site in Stratford where the Olympic stadium, village and aquatics centre would be based. England football legend Sir Bobby Charlton was at Wembley stadium to welcome the inspectors who also visited Wimbledon and Lord's cricket ground, the tennis and archery venues.

After London had faced severe criticism over transport in the IOC's first report on the bidding cities, one of the main goals was to show how the capital would be able to cope with transportation during the Olympics. It certainly helped that fewer people were using the city's roads and underground system because of the half-term holidays. But, in an inspired move, the commissioners were driven in Land Rovers down the tunnel built for the train link from the site of the Olympic complex in Stratford to King's Cross station to show how tens of thousands of spectators would travel to the Games by train once the link had been finished. The members were then transported to venues on an underground train covered in London 2012 logos. As they walked through one tube station they were greeted by an orchestra and messages on tannoys in several languages.

One of London 2012's biggest coups was to find a perfect spot overlooking the Olympic site at Stratford from which the inspectors would be able to observe. A special enclosed viewing platform was constructed at the top of a tower block, which is used as a residence for pensioners. From there the inspectors could see how close the Olympic complex was to the new Channel Tunnel Rail Link to King's Cross. More importantly they were able to get a perspective on London's plans, even on a cold dreary day in February. The site also looked busy with bulldozers already in action. Workmen were also in place at the Dome which was being transformed into a world-class indoor arena.

The London 2012 team were determined to show that plans for the Games were not just ideas on computerised images but they were already being implemented. The building of the aquatic centre was already in progress. The bid told the inspectors that several of the venues would be built, regardless of whether London won the Games. Lee explains the importance of this: 'We knew our rivals were putting it around that London was only a "virtual bid", that our ideas were only in computer graphics. This was a perfect way of dealing with this. The commission members saw that we were getting on with things.' Lee believes the decision to drive the commission members through the tunnel was one of the major successes of the visit. He says: 'Obviously it made for good pictures for the media, but it was important because we were addressing the key issue of transport where we had faced criticism from the IOC before. The tunnel was also a multi-billion pound project which was well under way and being delivered on time and to budget years before the Games. There were ten Land Rovers and two Commission members and staff in the back of each. We even made sure there were DVD players hanging from the front-seat headrests so that we could play some of the bid material during the journey. At the end of the day, there is only so much of a tunnel you can look at.'

On the third day commission members met Tony Blair at Downing Street together with then Opposition Leader Michael Howard and his then Liberal Democrat counterpart Charles Kennedy. Just a few months before a general election, the trio put on an unusual show of political solidarity for the bid. A buffet lunch at Number 10 was banned, however, since only one 'social occasion' was allowed under the IOC's ethics commission rules. That was reserved for Buckingham Palace in the evening where the Queen gave the commissioners the equivalent of a state visit.

They were ferried to Buckingham Palace from Canary Wharf along the Thames in the early evening, passing several landmarks illuminated with the 2012 logo, including Big Ben and the magnificent eighteenth-century façade of Somerset House. At the palace the commission members were escorted through the quadrangle, illuminated by torches, where they were serenaded by the Coldstream Guards string quartet. The Princess Royal greeted the commissioners before taking them to meet the Queen and the Duke of Edinburgh. By the time they were in the State Dining Room tucking into roast fillet of sea bass with wild mushrooms, breast of duck with bigarade sauce, braised chicory, snow peas (rather than 'mange tout'), rosti potatoes, salad and caramelised pear tart, they had been joined again by the Blairs, Chancellor Gordon Brown and a total of 46 guests from the world of Olympic and Paralympic sport in Britain. There appeared to be an effort made by the Palace not to use French at all at the function. The Queen stayed away from champagne and served the finest Sussex sparkling wine. The menus were also printed in English rather than the usual palace French. Palace aides said the Queen took a close personal interest in the dinner because – with only 46 guests – it was an intimate occasion by palace standards. The wines served came from New Zealand and Australia. There were no wines from the rivals countries – France, Spain or America.

Guests sat at one long table in the Dining Room. The Queen sat between commission chairwoman Nawal El Moutawakel and Sam Ramsamy. Further down the table sat Tony and Cherie Blair, Gordon Brown, Tessa Jowell, Richard Caborn, Ken Livingstone and Michael Howard amongst the other commissioners.

Four athlete ambassadors – Steve Redgrave, Denise Lewis, Jonathan Edwards and Dame Tanni Grey-Thompson – represented sport. It was a magnificent occasion which reminded the Olympic inspectors of the style and pageantry which Britain could bring to the Games.

When the commission members left the palace to the sound of bagpipes from the Irish guards, they were given a framed photograph taken before dinner of the group with the Queen. Each photograph was personally signed by the Queen, who went out onto the balcony to wave to the commissioners as they left.

Keith Mills explains: 'There were two Australian members of the commission who were republicans – Simon Balderstone and Bob Elphiniston. When they were given the signed photographs they got on the bus and said: "How are we going to explain this back in Oz?" But they worked very hard at the Palace. The image was certainly given to the members that London really wanted this.' Cherie Blair says: 'The Queen did her bit as well, she really did. At one point we had a quiet aside and she asked me "do you think we can win this?" And I told her yes and you could see she was excited by it. The Queen actually put herself out there and that is hugely impressive to people on the IOC.'

Coe was feeling confident that the visit had been a success. London 2012's leaders felt they had handled the initial concerns the IOC had expressed about transport. They had had the potential to become the Achilles heel of the bid. But by taking on the issue and showing IOC members at first hand how the transport would work, Coe and his team had solved the problem. The inspectors were left in no doubt that London could stage an excellent Games.

On the last day, the whole bid team, wearing branded 2012 coats and sweaters, went down to the Four Seasons Hotel to say goodbye to the commissioners who were leaving for Heathrow to fly straight to New York for their next inspection. 'After we waved goodbye and their coach left,' recalls Mike

Lee, 'there was a buoyant mood in the camp. We felt that the three and a half days could not have gone better, from the transport of the members around the city to the magnificent event at Buckingham Palace, which even included the Queen's wave from the Palace's main balcony.' The military-style preparation and planning led by bid chief operating officer Mike Power had worked.

Once the commission's visits were over, the challenge for all five bidding cities for the final five months of the campaign was to intensify both their lobbying and the international promotion of their bids. Mike Lee and his team ran by far the most proactive and robust campaign and London chased headlines more than any of its rivals. In addition to increasing interest in the bid abroad through interviews with foreign journalists, London 2012 needed to generate a series of expressions of support at home which could be communicated to the IOC. London 2012 knew that the opinion polls conducted the previous November by the IOC, which would appear in the evaluation commission report, would show lower levels of support from the public for London than would be shown for either Paris or Madrid. The British public take a much more cynical view of the world than many of their European counterparts. But London needed to show that support for the bid was increasing every day in the run-up to the vote. Supported by the East London boroughs, Transport for London and the bid's Nations and Regions Group, the team put in place a 'Back the Bid' campaign – including a series of posters, asking people to click on the London 2012 website or send text messages showing their support for the Games to come to London, emphasising the importance of national pride. In the end the campaign delivered more than three million registered supporters from the website, texts and the EDF Energy sponsored 'leapometer'. In fact all of the bid's premier corporate sponsors, which also included Virgin Atlantic, British Airways, BT and Accenture used their customer bases to increase registration. As the numbers grew there could now be no doubting growing support from the British public.

This energetic campaigning contrasted with the tactics of the Paris bid. The French were extremely cautious about virtually everything they did. This approach had its roots in meetings Mayor Bertrand Delanoe and Sports Minister Jean-François Lamour are said to have held with senior IOC figures before the start of the bid. The French were allegedly advised that there was a lot of goodwill towards Paris after the capital had failed twice before to get the 1992 and 2008 Games. Delanoe and Lamour were advised to run a very careful and safe campaign. 'There is no need to be aggressive,' they were told. 'If you are careful you will be in good shape.'

Paris 2012 chiefs would never admit in public that they were favourites but, certainly, they believed that they had a superb chance of winning if they kept their noses clean. This meant high-risk initiatives were off the agenda. The Paris communications campaign mirrored that outlook. Paris certainly did not chase big headlines in France or internationally; they concentrated on telling foreign journalists about the technical aspects of the bid and on the advantage of having the Stade de France in place. Their goal was to provide the 'mood music' to support the lobbying. They were successful in attracting stories about Paris in countries like Sweden, Canada, China and Italy. The bid's finest hour was the Champs Élysées festival of sport, pictures of which were carried on major international newspapers around the world. But, in general, the Paris media relations were low key.

In the end the approach was too cautious and Paris 2012 officials were not flexible enough. The Paris bid spent so much time worrying about what to do about an issue that they ended up not reacting to it properly. This safety-first approach was to backfire on Paris when the campaign reached its climax in Singapore in the final 72 hours before the vote. London would take full advantage of their failure to seize the day.

Mike Lee would have found it difficult to work for the Paris bid. He was at his best when having to chase a rival and create an interesting eye-catching narrative. Lee knew there were times when it was important not to over-hype a story but the notion of playing safety-first all the time was not in his DNA. This is a man who learned his PR skills in the sometimes ruthless world of Westminster politics. Giving up a top job at UEFA for a short-term contract at the bid was a risk for Lee. He simply had to try everything to make it a success.

London 2012 had to stay in the news in Britain to satisfy the hunger of the media and to keep up public awareness of the campaign. Increasing support at home was vital to London 2012. The communications team launched initiatives like the '2012 babies campaign' which involved parents of children born on 20 December 2004 having a chance to register for their children to be part of the cultural ceremonies at the London Games. At first sight these kinds of campaigns appear to have little significance. But Lee and his team knew that London 2012 had to be constantly in the newspapers to increase interest in the bid among the British public and to generate stories which reinforced the bid's key messages, particularly on legacy and the next generation. That meant being on the news pages as well as in the sports sections. Coe believed Britain could easily show as much passion as the French and Spanish for the Games as the vote got closer. When the IOC members travelled to Singapore, they would need to know that enthusiasm for the Games was increasing dramatically in Britain.

International rather than national PR became increasingly important in the last few months before the vote. Lee's PR team fostered good relations with key opinion-formers like Ed Hula, the editor of the Olympic newsletter *Around the Rings*, which is read by many IOC members. The communications team was regularly on the phone to the Olympic correspondents of the most influential international news agencies – Associated Press, Reuters and Agence France Presse. Their stories were read all around the world in numerous languages and therefore could reach the breakfast tables of IOC members across the globe.

Lee says: 'We had to be dynamic because we were not going to come from behind and beat Paris and Madrid by playing safe. The whole campaign about the babies born on 20.12 was a message reinforcing that our bid was about the next generation. It was all part of the jigsaw. I think Paris were very conservative in their PR. I felt that, despite their denials they

Left Barbara Cassani, chairman, and Simon Clegg, chief executive of the British Olympic Association, officially declare London's bid for the 2012 Olympic Games on the South Bank of the Thames with a backdrop of Tower Bridge. © Empics

Below The first hint that London might be gaining on the other bid cities – the official launch of the bid at London's Royal Opera House in January 2004: Seb Coe, Tony Blair, Barbara Cassani and Tessa Jowell. © Empics

Bottom Though the party at the London Eye was to celebrate being named one of the shortlisted cities, Barbara Cassani had privately made the decision to step down and had suggested Seb Coe as her successor. © Getty Images

Above Ken Livingstone, Cherie Blair and Jack Straw all pledge their support for the 2012 Games. © Empics

Left Mike Lee with Cherie Blair at the 2004 Athens Games.

Left The Secretary of State and chairman of the bid with the submission of the full bid document for London 2012 in November 2004. © Empics

One of the main issues for Mike Lee was the public relations of the bid and perceived lack of support from the public. The team went all out to change that:

Right Seb Coe with young athletes, Sally Conway, Kamran Panjavi and Tony Cesay.
© Empics

Right Record breaking yachtswoman Dame Ellen MacArthur signs the giant Make Britain Proud flag. © Empics

Below Olympic heptathlon champion Denise Lewis with babies born on 20.12 (20 December 2004), who will all play a part in the London Games.
© Eddie Mulholland/ Rex Features

Left Members of the Evaluation Commission visit Number 10 Downing Street in February 2005. Here Moroccan hurdler Nawal El Moutawakel meets Tony Blair, Seb Coe, Tessa Jowell and Mike Lee. © Getty/AFP

Left Much of the Commission's visit centred around the Olympic park in East London and its construction, whether the bid was successful or not. The construction workers later also got to meet Her Majesty Queen Elizabeth II.
© Getty Images

Below Mike Lee and his son meet boxer Amir Khan at the Lord Mayor's Parade in 2004.

Above left Tony Blair's visit to Singapore was one of the main surprises and successes of the bid. He used the time to meet IOC members, but also to visit a British school in the city. © Empics

Above right David Beckham and Tony and Cherie Blair – 'British brands' – who all helped win votes in the final crucial days before the vote. © Empics

Middle right Mike Lee, Seb Coe and IOC member and BOA chairman Craig Reedie at an essential press conference in advance of the vote. © Getty Images

Bottom right The London 2012 Communications Team.

Above left Regeneration and legacy shown through London 2012's use of 30 East London school-children. Amber Charles had delivered the London bid book to Lausanne in November 2004.
© Getty/AFP

Above right Princess Anne, Olympian and IOC member, makes her speech during London's presentation.
© Getty/Images

Right Tessa Jowell shares a joke with IOC President Jacques Rogge.
© Getty/AFP

Right Finally bid chairman Seb Coe is presented with the Host City Contract.
© Getty/Images

Above Double Olympic champion Daley Thompson celebrates London 2012's win with the schoolchildren who'd played such a big part. © Getty/AFP

Below Olympians Dame Kelly Holmes and Steve Cram lead the celebrations in London's Trafalgar Square . . .
© Julian Makey/Rex Features

Below . . . joined by thousands of ecstatic Britons in Trafalgar Square and elsewhere.
© Empics

Above The London 2012 team enjoy their win at the waterfront in Singapore. © Getty/AFP

Below Once the bid is won, the real work begins. Olympians past and present launch a lottery project to raise money for the Games. © Empics

Above Though London's official celebrations had to be delayed after tragedy struck the capital, acrobats and bunting adorned Nelson's Column in an amazing show in September 2005. © Empics

were not the favourites, they had got enough signals that they were front-runners and they did not want to disturb the waters.'

Proactive campaigns also have their risks, however. It is easy to tiptoe around a swimming pool but it is hard to jump in without making a splash. Inevitably London's creative campaign made some waves in some of the more conservative parts of the IOC and a showdown with the Lausanne body and its ethics commission was inevitable at some stage.

Paquerette Girard-Zapelli, the French judge in charge of the IOC's ethics commission, had policed the campaign very closely, much to the frustration of many of the bids, who were often unsure what they were and were not allowed to do as far as contact with IOC members was concerned. All the bidding cities had informers who tipped them off about what their rivals were doing. Girard-Zapelli regularly faced a barrage of complaints about cities breaking the lobbying rules. Most cities would not directly accuse a rival of cheating. They would simply ask the ethics commission a question like 'Is it OK to do this or that because I notice that it is being done in London, Madrid, Paris . . .' Girard-Zapelli, an attractive judge in her fifties, was rarely seen, at least in public, with a smile on her face for the whole of the campaign.

The IOC had got so fed up with the constant bickering that in December 2004, Rogge had been forced to call all the bid leaders to a meeting and tell them to treat each other with more respect. 'I am not happy with the atmosphere,' he told Coe and his counterparts. The bickering behind the scenes was inevitable, however. The IOC's rules were regarded by many as being too strict. Many IOC members thought there was nothing wrong with organised trips being set up to visit cities. They were being asked to make a decision which would lead to the IOC handing over hundreds of millions of pounds to a winning city and they felt they needed to see for themselves whether the city was capable of staging the Games. Bidding cities in their turn thought it was ridiculous that buying a cup of coffee for an IOC member was against the rules. The rules on advertising and promotion of bids internationally were also particularly tight.

No bid chiefs were prepared to go public with their criticism of the system for fear of damaging their campaigns. But Michael Payne, the IOC's former marketing director who has watched bidding campaigns closely for decades, echoed many of their views when he accused the IOC of being far too exacting in the middle of the campaign. Payne said: 'The IOC needs to walk the fine line between encouraging a city to bid and be creative and not suffocating the bidding process.' Payne remembered the early Samaranch days when few cities wanted to bid for the Games. He feared those days could return if cities felt they could not get some benefit from the campaign in terms of publicity for their city.

He continued: 'You do not address the excesses of some years ago by micro-managing the current rules process. Ways must be found to make the campaign beneficial to all the bidders. The most dangerous thing for the Olympic movement would be a return to the situation with just one or two cities bidding for the Games.'

But the IOC continued with their strict policing of the race. With just over two months to go before the vote, London's proactive and agenda-setting campaign got them into serious trouble with both IOC President Jacques Rogge and the ethics commission. Mike Lee and Seb Coe faced another crisis in Berlin.

Before the fall of the Berlin Wall, the Inter-Continental Hotel was at the heart of the more lively side of the German capital. Visitors to West Berlin would love to stay close to the shops and restaurants on the Kurfürstendamm Street – or 'Ku-damn' as it is known to the locals. The hotel was within a minute's walk of the Kaiser-Wilhelm Memorial church with its famous cut-off spire which was destroyed in World War Two. But the eastern part of Berlin has always been the most attractive side of the city architecturally. After the Wall fell in 1989 and modern shops, restaurants and bars returned to the land occupied by the communists, the Kurfürstendamm lost some of its sparkle and more and more visitors to Berlin were lured to the east. The Inter-Continental, next to the huge gardens of the Berlin Zoo, is still a luxury hotel with excellent conference facilities but the attractions nearby are not as great as they were. In that way it was a perfect venue for the SportAccord Olympic conference in April 2005, one of the most important meetings before the Singapore vote.

The annual conference brought together sports business experts and the Presidents of the international sports federations. For five days delegates locked themselves away in the lobbies and conference rooms of the hotel and talked about very little apart from Olympic politics. German was hardly heard in the hotel and, apart from the country's famous beer being served at the bar, the Inter-Continental was turned into 'Olympic soil' which could have been anywhere in the world.

Each city had an opportunity to give a presentation to the meeting of international sports federations and each city had its own exhibition stand outside the conference room. Moscow caused a stir by hiring glamour girls from a model agency to look after its stand. But the most interesting action was around the bar in the lobby. Coe, Keith Mills, Craig Reedie and Debbie Jevans would often be seen in deep conversations with IOC members. During the day Coe would regularly sit in the hotel's café outside giving a series of interviews to international journalists. Mike Lee's job in the first 24 hours was to satisfy the demands of the international media for Coe, whose opinions are often sought on athletics and Olympic affairs. But his mind was on other things: London was preparing to launch a major initiative in the campaign that was hoped to be a great coup.

It all started seemingly harmlessly on the Sunday, the first full day of the conference, when Seb Coe and the London team gave a presentation to the delegates, which set out a charter of promises to the international sports federations. These included assurances that each technical delegate from each sport would be given free accommodation and living expenses to stay in London for up to a year before the Games to oversee preparations. All personnel accredited by international federations would also receive a discount card, offering reductions of between 20 and 50 per cent at selected restaurants, shops and theatres.

New York was also offering free marketing advice to all sports federations to develop their sport if the Games went to the Big Apple. But then London launched another charter with another series of guarantees. It contained dozens of promises worth around £15 million which London would provide if they won the right to stage the 2012 Games. These included a $50,000 or £30,000 credit to all 200 national Olympic committees towards the cost of a UK training base, free full-fare flexible air tickets, train travel plus £60 worth of phone calls for all 10,500 athletes.

The package was simply aimed at solving many of the problems international sports federations or national teams face at the Olympics. It was not new for a host city to provide free plane tickets for athletes, for example, but by offering a flexible fare, athletes would avoid past situations where they had been forced to fly a particular airline or a particular route to get to the Games. This had led to long trips and the last thing a competitor wants to do before the Games is spend too much time on a plane or in an airport lounge waiting for a transfer. The package was well received by many international sports federation Presidents who felt London 2012 leaders were showing that they knew what they were talking about in the organisation of the Games.

The charters in general were aimed at neutralising similar initiatives from London's rivals. Keith Mills explains: 'We knew from other bidding races that other cities had pulled something out of the bag in the run-up to the votes, like Sydney offering free flights to Australia. We wanted to pre-empt any of the other cities pulling goodies out of the bag in the last eight weeks. We wanted to neutralise the competition. We knew there were risks but it was a risk worth taking.'

But Rogge, who was chairing a meeting of his ruling executive board in Berlin during the conference, was not amused. The IOC President saw the package as a series of sweeteners and a vote-grabbing stunt. Paquerette Girard-Zapelli was soon dispatched to start investigating the charters to see if they broke the bidding rules. London 2012's initiative became the talk of the Inter-Continental Hotel. London's rivals were taken by surprise by them and, while accepting that they were a brilliant idea, the other cities knew the British were sailing close to the wind.

It was not long before Rogge was expressing his views in a breakfast briefing with the leading IOC-beat journalists in Berlin. He warned all the cities about stunts in the final eleven weeks of campaigning and stated that any city which announced a fundamental change to the details of its bid books submitted the previous November would be told to withdraw it. He did not want a 'bidding war' or a return to the days of the Salt Lake scandal. The London bid felt that offering money to ensure competitors got to the Games in better physical and mental shape was hardly the same as providing a free university education for an IOC member's son or daughter or offering an Olympic delegate cash, but Rogge said: 'All of a sudden people start throwing money through the windows. We are coming from a period of excess and red carpet treatment. We don't want a repeat of that.'

Rogge's comments turned the issue into a huge story. The danger for London was that this would develop into a full-scale ethics commission investigation that would be hugely damaging to the bid. Anything that brought back the memories of the Salt Lake scandal to IOC members had the potential to sink the bid. Mike Lee soon realised London had to act quickly to stop the charters turning into a crisis. 'It soon became clear that the charters were turning into a huge problem for us.' All the five cities had been called into a meeting with Girard-Zapelli and told for the first time that they could not offer anything that was not in the candidate files.

He explains: 'Back at bid headquarters the lawyers started trawling through the bid book to check the references to the charter proposals. Some of the ideas were contained in the bid book but it is true that there were only tenuous links to some of the other proposals. It was decided that we could have won a legal battle with the IOC on this but, at this stage of the campaign, it was clearly not a good idea. The question was: how did we best get out of the situation?

'Seb and Keith had to leave Berlin for bid business back in London, but a few of us remained behind. I was able to meet with Rogge's chief of staff Christophe de Kepper. I knew him from my UEFA days when we worked together on an international campaign to get the European Union to give sport a special status in law. He made it clear to me that Jacques Rogge was very unhappy. Debbie Jevans and I then had coffee with Australian IOC member Kevan Gosper to seek more advice. Gosper said that we had to get out of the situation as quickly as possible. Seb, Keith and I stayed in phone contact and we all agreed this was serious and we needed to act. After another conversation with de Kepper, we decided that we had to withdraw the charters. It was important to show the IOC that we could act decisively and quickly.

'We did take a lot of criticism for the whole issue by people who wrongly regarded the charters as a PR stunt. A leading columnist from the *Daily Telegraph* called for my resignation live on BBC radio on the Sunday after the conference finished. I remember choking on my coffee when I heard that. The fact was that the charters were not just a PR strategy – they had been developed to show our interest in meeting the needs of the athletes and officials. For about 48 hours there was loads of media fallout but over the week we turned that round and by the following Sunday we had media pieces applauding our strategy. I don't think Berlin damaged us in the end because we got out from the conflict quickly and the charters showed the international sports federations and national Olympic committees that we recognised many of their concerns.'

The spring of 2005, therefore, saw a huge acceleration in the pace of the 2012 campaign. It was rapidly turning into a three-city contest between Paris, London and Madrid.

London and Madrid were catching up the French as the vote got closer and London was, by far, the city with the most momentum, thanks to the creative communications and lobbying campaigns. More importantly, Baudillon's emotional attack on Mike Lee with just over a month to go suggested the French were getting nervous about London's momentum. And the London 2012 team was secretly planning to launch something even more powerful before the vote on 6 July.

9. HITTING THE HOME STRAIGHT

While purple-necked peacocks calmly roamed the immaculate lawns of his tranquil, tropical retreat near Singapore, Sebastian Coe looked relaxed as he ordered a glass of iced water and made himself comfortable on a sofa in the open-air Pavilion lounge. The suits and ties he had worn constantly during his travels around the world in the previous two months were hanging in the wardrobe of his hotel room, granted a rare few days off from the gruelling hours of Olympic lobbying.

To the rest of the wealthy guests at Sentosa Island's Beaufort Hotel, the double Olympic champion looked, at first glance, like a normal western tourist in his open-necked shirt and dark trousers. The only puzzle was that, apart from the odd dip in the outdoor swimming pool and a daily massage, this particular guest did not appear to be taking advantage of the hotel's mud pools and steam baths, the two championship golf courses or the nearby Tanjong Beach with its white sand and palm trees. To the other guests, it must have seemed crazy for anybody to come to this five-star hideaway hotel and spend most of the time locked away in a room mysteriously guarded by security men.

But Coe and twenty senior figures from his London 2012 team had chosen the tranquillity of Sentosa for a special reason in the last week before the Singapore vote.

The lobbying teams of the other bidding cities had rushed straight to the bustle of the International Olympic Committee's Raffles Hotel complex in central Singapore in the last week of June. They were determined not to miss the chance to talk to IOC members who were arriving early for the Olympic meetings, which were due to start with a meeting of the IOC's ruling executive board on 2 July.

London 2012 had posted several 'spotters' in the Raffles Hotel to keep an eye open for IOC delegates checking-in early. But Coe, Keith Mills, Craig Reedie and Mike Lee had taken the London 2012 team into hiding for the final week before the IOC session. It was an unusual decision and some might have seen it as a gamble for the bid's major players to stay away from the Raffles for a few days. But it was to turn out to be an inspired piece of planning.

From his running days Coe knew the importance of pre-Olympic training camps where athletes focus completely on the competition ahead without any distractions. Sentosa Island was perfect. Although it was only twenty minutes by taxi from the centre of Singapore, it was a world away from the city's skyscrapers and busy streets. The island is a former British fortress which was used as a military base until 1967 when it was handed back to the Singaporean government. It was then turned into a holiday resort and given a new name which means 'peace and tranquillity' in Malay. Nearly three-quarters of the 500-hectare island is covered in rain forest inhabited by monkeys, peacocks and parrots. The rest is long white, sandy beaches. At the end of June, humidity levels are high and temperatures are way into the 30s (centigrade). So rest and relaxation is on most people's agenda. The guests in the Beaufort spend their days swimming with dolphins, lazing on sandy beaches or trying to hit a golf ball away from ponds and pools.

Craig Reedie, an accomplished golfer with a handicap of seven, would love to have slipped his golf shoes on for a few hours on Sentosa. However, while a 'diplomatic game' was arranged for his wife Rosemary with Anne Rogge, the spouse of the IOC President, Reedie joined the London 2012 team in the guarded conference room. Rarely has so much secrecy surrounded a bidding team in the last ten days of a campaign.

Here Coe was preparing for one of the most emotional presentations ever to be made to a meeting of the International Olympic Committee. He was determined that neither London's rivals nor the media was going to get the tiniest sniff of it.

Nothing had been left to chance in the final fortnight of campaigning. Coe and Mills even travelled to Singapore in separate planes for safety reasons. In Sentosa they were protected from spying eyes by a Metropolitan police chief inspector, in-house security and an accreditation system which allowed only London 2012 staff to within eavesdropping distance of the speeches being rehearsed behind closed doors.

The reason for the secrecy was simple. London's intelligence was suggesting that many more IOC members than ever before were heading to Singapore still undecided about how they were going to vote. The presentations were therefore going to be more important than in any other bidding race. So Coe and his team had to make sure every sentence was well-chosen and every video would have an impact. The main scriptwriter, ex-journalist, Nick Varley, was permanently on hand and London even brought an editing unit with them to Sentosa to put the finishing touches to the films.

The timing of the Sentosa camp was crucial. Coe would have no time to look at the speeches or the videos after the following weekend when the team moved to the Raffles Hotel to begin the final lobbying. And, with few IOC members in town yet, it made sense to shake off the jetlag early and spend five days perfecting the 45-minute presentation.

The Sentosa trip was also about bonding and recharging batteries. Despite all the travelling in the previous six months, the London 2012 team would need to feel fresh when they stepped into the Raffles Hotel. Coe also wanted everybody to discuss tactics for the final few days of campaigning when every hour needed to be well used to get votes. This was far easier away from the media spotlight.

As he sat in the Pavilion lounge looking out at the lily-covered ponds and multi-coloured flower beds, Coe felt a certain amount of satisfaction at how far the bid had come in the eleven months since the troubled days of the *Panorama* débâcle. Certainly huge progress had been made in the technical side of the bid since May 2004 when London's plans were criticised by the IOC's first report on the 2012 cities.

In the IOC assessment of May 2004, the railways in London were described as 'often obsolete'. The report said 'considerable investments' would have to be made to upgrade the existing system in terms of capacity and safety. But the London team had spent a lot of time explaining to both the evaluation commission and IOC members how the new Channel Tunnel Rail Link from King's Cross station to Stratford would allow spectators to travel from central London into the Olympic complex. Shuttle trains would run around the clock during the Games and the Olympic Park would be served by ten different rail lines with the upgrading of underground, light rail and regional rail networks in east London.

The evaluation commission report published just three weeks before the team travelled to Singapore gave the capital's transport and infrastructure solid marks and stated that London would be 'capable of coping with Games-time traffic'.

The commission was even more positive about the transport in Paris, saying the French capital would cope 'comfortably' with traffic during the Games. But what mattered was that London's opponents had always seen transport as the bid's Achilles heel. Now the IOC was telling its members that transport in London was no longer a negative issue. Coe realised this was a huge leap forward and gave a certain IOC HQ blessing to London's work.

The cities were not rated in any order in the commission's analysis. But close reading of the report suggested that, while Paris received the best technical report, London and Madrid were close behind. Moscow and New York were now regarded as outsiders.

New York was slipping further behind because of a row over its main stadium on the west side of Manhattan. Less than 24 hours after the evaluation commission report was published on 6 June, New York State's Public Authorities refused to approve funding of £163.6 million towards the £1.2 billion cost of the main stadium on the west side of Manhattan. For a few days there were fears that New York would have to make an embarrassing withdrawal from the bidding race. Without a main stadium, the bid would become a laughing stock. Amazingly, within just a week, Mayor Michael Bloomberg and his deputy Dan Doctoroff negotiated a deal to use another new stadium across the East River in Queens. But the arena, to be used afterwards by the Mets baseball team, was outside of Manhattan and the dream of having the Games at the heart of the Big Apple had gone.

In the end, it was the Americans' calamitous west side story that destroyed their bid.

It was not hard to see that Paris was definitely the evaluation commission's favourite. In fact the report was full of so many glowing adjectives for France's plans that there were mumblings in the Olympic world and in the media in the final weeks before Singapore that the city had been given too much of an easy ride. Some observers were suggesting that the excellent Paris showing might even help London because it boosted the conspiracy theory that the IOC administration wanted the French to win.

There was a general belief that some IOC members would not like the idea of being told what to do by Lausanne. Lee was determined that the London 2012 bid would not get dragged into commenting on any of those rumours, however. He knew it was normal for conspiracy theories to do the rounds in the build-up to a vote. He also knew it was important not to attach too much importance to them.

Lee says: 'We were pleased with the outcome of the evaluation commission report. We had spent a lot of time on the technical plans since the first report from the IOC had criticised transport. There was no point running away from those comments. We had directly addressed them and there were now no clear weaknesses in London's bid in the final report, particularly as far as transport and political support were concerned. We felt we had established a really sound technical basis for the final push towards Singapore.

'In general we did feel very satisfied that the report provided the IOC with a rational case to bring the Games to London. It gave us a platform on which to build our vision for the presentation in Singapore – to move from the rational to the emotional.'

Despite Philippe Baudillon's worries about London's communications tactics, the mood in the Paris camp was still definitely high when their bid team touched down in Singapore and headed straight to the Raffles Hotel. Baudillon was still talking modestly in public. But privately, the French had analysed their level of support carefully and they believed they had enough votes to win. The French were convinced that, barring a major gaffe, they would be over the line first by the evening of 6 July.

Coe was aware that the French were confident. But he was having no defeatist talk in Sentosa. This is a man who has a reputation in the Olympic world for showing courage in adversity. Coe was at his best when others were writing him off. As far as he was concerned, nothing was decided until the members started pressing their electronic voting buttons. The 2012 race was still too close to call and London had 'everything to play for' in the presentations.

Usually IOC members know pretty well how they are going to vote before they listen to each city's 45-minute sales pitch. The accepted wisdom in the Olympic world is that a city can lose votes from a bad presentation but a bid rarely snatches victory on the strength of a few good speeches alone. But Coe had a gut instinct that the 2012 race was going to be very different. Tessa Jowell had come back from a meeting with one influential Olympic figure, saying she had been told that London needed to show real passion in the presentation. London was getting the message from many IOC members that the presentations were going to be crucial.

It was all music to the ears of Coe and Lee who had been working hard with the bid team on the narrative of London 2012's vision. Coe had already decided that he was going to talk about how watching the 1968 Mexico Olympics on a flickering black-and-white TV set in a school hall in Sheffield had first opened a 'window on a new world' for him and, for that, he owed a debt of gratitude to the movement. He had rehearsed the emotional memory during a speech to British sports and local government officials at a conference at

Westminster soon after he was appointed chairman of the bid and had told the story so well that some people in the audience immediately suggested it should be part of the Singapore presentation. But the London 2012 leader had something even more powerful up his sleeve.

The films bidding cities show to IOC members are usually like tourist information trailers with some sport and ethnic diversity thrown in. Bids show off their most famous tourist attractions, their best stadia and the faces of children in their city from all over the world. IOC members have seen scores of these films over the years. And many members switch off when they appear on the screen in front of them.

London could have produced one of these films easily. But Coe, Lee and David Magliano were preparing to break the mould in terms of Olympic campaigning. Having watched scores of previous bid presentations at Canary Wharf during their Wednesday night viewings, they were determined to do something dramatically different in their final pitch to the IOC. On Sentosa, the London team was putting the finishing touches to the most emotional presentation ever to be shown to an IOC meeting.

Britain is the home of some of the most creative minds in the media industry. The London 2012 campaign was never short of powerful images in its videos or posters. The bid produced a high-tech film early on in the campaign about the sports venues, presented by the BBC's Sue Barker. It was very matter-of-fact and detailed, but it brought alive the attractive plans for beach volleyball at Horse Guards Parade and marathons and triathlon races past London's famous landmarks.

But the London 2012 team also wanted something lighter to show IOC members during the campaign. The UK was famous for its humour and, working to the London team's brief, the New Moon production company, led by director Daryl Goodrich and producer Caroline Rowland, put together a clever film called 'Sport at Heart'. It was a slick and genuinely witty film, crammed with celebrities such as David Beckham and Roger Moore, famous landmarks and ordinary people inspired to flex their sporting muscles as young female athlete Jo Ankier, a British steeplechaser, passed them on a run around London set to the bid's soundtrack song *Proud* by vocalist Heather Small.

A scene with Roger Moore as James Bond being handed a briefcase by Miss Moneypenny outside the headquarters of MI5 containing a banana and sandwiches always got a laugh when it was aired. But it was also a clever way of reminding IOC members about Britain's solid record on security. The film subsequently won thirteen prizes at the International Visual Communications Awards.

The stakes were raised much higher in the build-up to Singapore, however. It emerged that London's rivals were calling in big guns from the film world to produce their videos. Hollywood directors Luc Besson and Steven Spielberg were working on the Paris and New York films respectively. Daryl Goodrich, a 40-year-old from Bradford, could not claim to be in their class, having never directed a feature film. But after the success of 'Sport at Heart' he was happy to team up again with Caroline Rowland to support London's final push. Faced with a demanding brief and short timescales, Goodrich and Rowland had thought long and hard about the best way in which to show how Olympic champions are produced from a broad base of children participating in sport and to use film to bring alive the concept of inspiring young people into sport.

It was no surprise that the film they eventually produced, called 'Inspiration', was kept under lock and key on Sentosa. It was revolutionary in terms of Olympic bidding. For the first time, a city was preparing to make a pitch that had more in common with a general election campaign than an Olympic bidding race. The story showed four children from Mexico, Africa, Russia and China watching images of a London Games in 2012 and being inspired to leave behind life on the streets or distractions at home to follow the Olympic dream. In the second half of the film the youngsters go on to become a successful Olympic cyclist, runner, swimmer and gymnast. In one way, the idea was a gamble: some people were sure to ask the question why a London Games would be any better at helping to solve the problem than any other city. But London 2012's team knew they had the answer to that question and would stress that the capital was a magnet to the youth of the world. There were risks involved but Coe knew he had to take them to beat Paris. Playing safe was not an option.

The budget for 'Inspiration' was around £400,000, a fraction of the money made available to Besson. While the Hollywood director travelled to Singapore to promote the film, the New Moon team kept quiet about their emotional film. Coe did not want to give London's rivals any idea of what his team was preparing.

All the London speakers rehearsed and reworked their speeches time and time again in the conference room on Sentosa. Coe, Craig Reedie, Ken Livingstone, Tessa Jowell and Denise Lewis were all preparing to speak to the IOC session. Magliano and Lee, working with Sara Donaldson of production company Live, and scriptwriter, Nick Varley, analysed every sentence they delivered. From speech delivery to body language, the team worked together to ensure that the delegation on the platform was sending out the right messages. Coe worked on getting over his passion across to the audience while Craig Reedie spent time perfecting his French pronunciation. The Scot has an accent which is more Perth than Perpignan, but Britain did not want to be accused of failing to speak in both official IOC languages – English and French.

Mike Lee says: 'We set up a full-scale rehearsal room and brought the Live production crew with us. The room had a lectern and we created a platform for those who would be sitting on the stage in Singapore. We also had an editing facility with us so that we could work on the films and trim them if we felt we were running out of time. We worked on everything. Over five days we spent a lot of time refining the scripts, the visual material and putting the finishing touches to the presentations. A lot of the time was focused on Seb's speech, which would form the final part of the presentation. The crucial final emotional push had to feel totally genuine. Seb worked to develop the draft and then he would test his changes on us. The words had, ultimately, to be his.

'It was a smart move to go to Sentosa. It gave us the opportunity to develop the presentations away from the limelight and to get it absolutely right before we went to Singapore when the pressure on us would be intense. There was a real training camp mentality in Sentosa. We knew we were working on something very special and Sentosa gave us focus. We were striving for perfection.'

Mills and Coe did not stay away from the Raffles Hotel completely during their stay on Sentosa. Now and again they would take a break from their work and make a quick visit to make contact with IOC members who had arrived early. The whole team packed their bags, however, on the weekend of 2 and 3 July, just three days before the vote, and moved their campaign to the Carlton Hotel, a minute's walk from the Raffles Hotel.

London 2012 planned to hold a series of media briefings in the final days before the vote when the communications campaign needed to pick up speed again, but they wanted the press conferences to be held away from the main IOC hotel. Ambassadors like David Beckham would attract a huge amount of media attention and it was important that the media frenzy did not get in the way of the work of IOC members – or indeed upstage them.

London had by far the highest profile for the media in the last days before the vote. Lee explains: 'The whole goal of the final seventy-two hours of the campaign was to join up the lobbying and the communications strategy. The communications team was determined that London 2012 would dominate the media landscape with a combination of high-profile press conferences and photo opportunities, allied to a strategy targeted at certain media outlets. We set a pace that none of the other bids could live with.'

Lee and his deputy Jackie Brock-Doyle had been working hard on the bid's relations with all the main Singapore newspapers and television stations. Many members would be reading the local English language newspapers over breakfast and it was important that there were plenty of stories about London. The London 2012 communications team had even researched in advance the channel numbers on the TV sets in the IOC members' bedrooms. Some of these were Singapore news channels and other Asian networks, followed by CNN and BBC World. The London team made sure these channels had plenty of access to London 2012 people and materials. Special interviews with the Princess Royal were broadcast around the clock as IOC members began checking into the hotel. Press conferences and photo opportunities with David

Beckham, Tony Blair and several of the other sporting ambassadors were also arranged in the final days before the vote. They dominated the media coverage.

The Princess Royal gave a rare press conference together with Ade Adepitan, the wheelchair basketball player who is also one of the stars of the BBC's promotional adverts – an intriguing combination for the media. Lee says: 'That press conference sent a clear message about Royal support for the bid, alongside the support of a young dreadlocked Paralympian. It symbolised London's commitment to Paralympic sport and showed a creative mix. We also held press conferences with the Prime Minister and Seb Coe, as well as our sporting ambassadors, and one to show stakeholder support with Ken Livingstone, Tessa Jowell and Craig Reedie. We had recorded clips with the Prime Minister and Seb Coe before we came to Singapore, which we made available for broadcast. We gave the Singapore channels, CNN, BBC World and the other Asian broadcasters plenty of access to our material. This was important because it all filtered through the Raffles Hotel complex. We were providing the perpetual background noise and showing that the London campaign had momentum. It was helping to set the scene for the private lobbying of IOC members.'

The high-profile strategy did have its risks, however. London could have got into trouble with the ethics commission just two days before the vote when Australian Olympic consultant Jim Sloman criticised the Stade de France at a London 2012 press conference, saying the Paris arena had problems staging athletics. Whilst the comments were justified by difficulties at the 2003 World Athletics Championships, bids are banned from criticising each other in public and Paris could have complained about the criticism. Interestingly, the French chose to turn the other cheek as a row would have further focused attention on some of the weaknesses of the Stade de France. Lee explains: 'No one could have quite predicted the comments Jim made but we knew his views and they were fair and not unhelpful. However once he put them on the record, it was important that the bid distanced itself from them. I made it clear that Jim was not being paid by London 2012 but he was entitled to his views. In the end the effect was that the comments did draw attention to an underlying concern about the Stade de France. Whilst it was a difficult afternoon dealing with an excited media, the outcome was not without its benefits.'

There is no doubt that Paris PR man Jon Tibbs was getting increasingly worried that London 2012 was setting the media agenda and attracting far more coverage on the channels watched by IOC members. He claims that he tried to persuade Paris to organise more press conferences and media opportunities but the French yet again wanted to play safe. The Paris team were still confident that it had enough votes to win and they were determined not to make any mistakes. They had 'blind faith' in the advice they had received early on in the campaign that the IOC would finally reward Paris at their third time of bidding. They were unwilling to change their tactics at the last minute. As one seasoned Olympic observer said, 'The French went to steamy Singapore and froze. They could not agree how to handle the situation. They had been told to be very low key and they were determined to stick to that policy even when they were being advised to increase their media presence.' As a result London won the media battle in Singapore with ease.

'It was striking that while we knew they were actively lobbying in the hotel,' says Lee, 'Paris seemed to be virtually non-existent in other areas in the final days of the campaign. Their media activity was poor. But I had heard that their film was a big part of the Paris presentation. We were worried that they might have something special up their sleeves.'

There were plenty of people in Singapore who believed the French had got it just right. Like an athlete leading a race from the start, their plan was to keep going at the same predictable pace and keep their blinkers firmly on. Since most of the media were still predicting a Paris victory, many in the French camp felt there was still no need to worry. The French forgot, of course, that they were facing a team led by one of the greatest sprint finishers in Olympic history. Seb Coe had caught many a front-runner in the last few strides during his career on the track.

While Lee was concentrating on getting London 2012 on to TV and into the newspapers, Coe was spending quality time with one of London's rivals. The behind-the-scenes lobbying was witnessing dramatic days in the final 72 hours before the vote: Coe was spotted in the Ink Club Bar at the Raffles Hotel in the early hours of the morning with Juan Antonio Samaranch junior and Israel's IOC member Alex Gilady.

Gilady is a 63-year-old former TV commentator who is the eyes and ears of American TV in the IOC as a vice-president of the NBC Sports network, which owns the US rights for the Games. The affable IOC member is also a great fan of London, having had a home in the city for decades. More importantly, the Israeli is a close friend and loyal confidant of former IOC President Juan Antonio Samaranch.

It was already suspected that Juan Antonio Samaranch senior was heavily involved in the 2012 race and working hard behind the scenes to help Madrid. Although he no longer holds the same kind of influence in the IOC he enjoyed for twenty years as President, Samaranch is still a powerful figure who demands respect from many of his colleagues. The big question was: where would the Spanish city's support go in a London-Paris final round of voting? Coe was working hard with Madrid to make sure as much of it as possible would come to London.

It was a competitive game since France's lobbyists were also working behind the scenes to reach the same goal. But as the days went on, it became clear that Samaranch had a huge amount of respect for the London bid.

Coe maintains that there was no special deal with Madrid, however. He says; 'People don't vote in blocs in the IOC so nobody can deliver anything in that respect. There was no deal, other than a bond of friendship. He said to me that London had done well. But I had been friends with Samaranch and his son for years and I had spent a lot of time in Spain.'

The race between Paris and London was, therefore, pretty much neck-and-neck in those final days before the vote. The French were still confident that 'safety first' was working and that view was still shared by most of the media and many independent IOC experts. London, spurred on by its dominance of the communications campaign, was picking up momentum with every passing hour. Coe, Mills and Reedie were doing everything they could to put London closer to the line by shoring up the British vote in chats with IOC members.

But they knew the bid needed an extra turn of pace to outstrip the French in those final hours before the vote. They turned to two of the most famous Britons on the planet to provide it.

10. BECKHAM AND BLAIR

David Beckham walked into the drinks party at the Esplanade Concert Hall looking smart in his light-brown London 2012 suit and stripy multicoloured tie. A few heads turned but there was no grand stage-managed entrance for the England football captain.

This was an informal opportunity for the delegations of the five bid teams to mingle with voting Olympic leaders before the opening ceremony of the IOC Session in the theatre. Tickets were hard to come by for the event at the waterfront theatre, an unusual, futuristic building which dominates central Singapore with two domes that, from a distance, look like huge metal tea-strainers. Victoria Beckham stayed back at the couple's luxury hotel suite and the footballer joined the rest of the British sports stars acting as ambassadors for the bid.

Beckham is a sporting icon in Asia where English football is followed closely on satellite TV and his former club Manchester United have hundreds of thousands of fans. The thirty-year-old faced the ubiquitous scrum of photographers when he came into the building. But he was now on safe ground, away from autograph-hunting fans and the excited 'snappers' in an area policed by security guards. He began chatting quietly with Britain's former Olympic competitors, including heptathlete Denise Lewis, rower Sir Steve Redgrave and triple jumper Jonathan Edwards. But the peace did not last long.

Beckham had hardly had time to take a glass of water from the waitress's tray before two excited ladies in their twenties rushed up to him, holding out pens and their IOC ceremony programmes in anticipation of an autograph. Catching sight of the Paris 2012 bid badges on their jackets and listening to their French accents, the England captain smiled politely and signed the programmes. The irony of the moment was immeasurable. Even though the French were understood to be far from happy with London 2012 playing its trump 'celebrity card' in Singapore, some of their bid team were clearly delighted to be a few steps away from a global superstar. They were not alone.

Members of the Madrid bid delegation soon spotted the midfielder. Within a minute, a queue started to form in front of a man who started his life in obscurity in East London's Leytonstone before bursting into Manchester United's first team, marrying one of the Spice Girls and becoming one of the most recognisable faces on the planet. Beckham and his wife have sometimes been accused of seeking too much publicity. This is the downside of their fame. Even among sports stars and officials on duty for their Olympic bids, the Real Madrid star cannot relax and enjoy a quiet drink without being surrounded by adoring fans. There must be few public places on the planet where Beckham can walk, sit or stand without being approached.

Yet, it was in the middle of this wild adoration in Singapore that another side of the England captain, rarely seen in public, came to light. As more and more people tried to get close to the player, a waitress lost control of her tray and a glass crashed to the floor. Beckham immediately stopped signing autographs, bent down and picked up the pieces of glass and handed them to her with a smile. It was the kind of diplomacy and style that they teach in British embassies around the world. It certainly wasn't the behaviour of a prima donna footballer. It didn't match some people's perception of Beckham from the occasions when, earlier in his career, he had lost his cool on the pitch under duress.

After the ceremony, a buffet was served to the IOC members and bid officials. Realising that he was in danger of attracting too much attention in front of the members, Beckham did not stay for long. 'It's probably best if I go now,' he whispered to Denise Lewis and apologised to the other fellow sporting ambassadors for his early departure. Maybe Beckham was just keen to get back to Victoria at the hotel and go for dinner. Maybe he felt uncomfortable in unfamiliar surroundings. Maybe he was simply bored after a long ceremony which reached a fairly surreal climax with the 'baptism' of a new orchid flower called 'Vanda IOC'. But the England captain also clearly understood that it was not his job to steal the show.

Mike Lee, experienced in dealing with top sportspeople during his days working for the European football governing body UEFA and the English Premier League, was particularly impressed by the style of the England captain throughout the trip to Singapore. 'Some people thought it was a mistake to bring Beckham to the vote in Singapore. They said there would be too much fuss around him and that any media scrums would upset IOC members, especially since he is not an Olympian. The last thing we wanted to do was upset the very IOC members whose support we needed. We didn't want them saying Beckham was just a gimmick who was turning their hotel into a madhouse.

'We did everything we could to stop a media circus building up around him in the IOC environment in Singapore. We were very careful in choosing the points where he made his public appearances.

'Everything David does attracts ferocious media interest. In Asia it is almost unbelievable and sometimes frightening. Yet he always maintained a good humour. He was highly impressive. He seems to have a natural understanding of what is appropriate in a particular situation.'

This is a lesser-known side of Beckham's character. He is often seen in British newspapers and magazines with his wife, walking into expensive restaurants wearing the latest fashionable clothes; he is regularly portrayed by TV impressionists and comedians as monosyllabic and lacking in intellectual depth – a simple man who lives the classic superstar's life with its glamorous women, nightclubs and celebrity parties. Mike Lee believes Beckham is a far more intelligent, modest and mature figure than this public image suggests.

England football manager Sven-Goran Eriksson helped to persuade Beckham to go to Singapore after he was approached with the request by Sports Minister Richard Caborn and his friend and adviser Dave Richards, the English Premier League chairman. Part of the deal was that Eriksson, who has always been amazingly loyal to Beckham during periods when he has been out of form, also acted as an ambassador in Singapore.

Beckham's role in the bid's public relations was cleverly positioned – the East London boy who became a massive star through sport. He fitted in perfectly to the bid's campaign to stress the importance of the Olympics to the regeneration of that part of London and of sport's crucial role in helping children to fulfil their dreams.

Lee says: 'Beckham was on holiday before the IOC meeting and he cut the whole thing short to take part. The day before he made his first public appearance, he and Victoria celebrated their wedding anniversary in Singapore. Because of his popularity in Asia, they couldn't even leave the hotel where they were staying and spent the whole day there.

'When he attended a reception at the British High Commission, he mingled and talked to everybody but he was always very appropriate. It seemed important to David that he did not upstage the Olympians in the London bid. He realised they were the big players in the Olympic world and he wasn't. He was very much a guest in their world.

'He also didn't want pomp and circumstance around him. There is no doubt he has a certain modesty. At one point during the High Commission party, he said: "When Seb Coe has a moment, I'd just like to say hello." At our main sports press conference, he certainly did not want to be put ahead of any of the other sportspeople, especially five-times gold medal winner Steve Redgrave. Our platform speakers had 25 Olympic and Paralympic gold medals between them and even though many of the questions were being fired at David by the journalists, he was happy to step back and let others do the talking.

'David took nothing for granted. He was humble about things. Even when we won, having just escaped a crazy media scrum, he asked me politely, "Is it OK if Victoria and me come to the party tonight?"'

Lee believes Paris 2012 chiefs were very frustrated at being upstaged on the celebrity front and some Olympic observers believe that they started complaining behind the scenes ahead of Singapore, particularly as they appeared to be having difficulty in getting international stars to attend. Zinedine Zidane is a footballing great and had been part of the Paris bid for the 2008 Games but Beckham's Real Madrid teammate and Paris ambassador was unable to make the trip. In the end the most high-profile French footballer who went to Singapore was Laurent Blanc, part of the 1998 World Cup-winning team but hardly a household name across the world.

It was nothing new for bidding cities to bring big names from sport or entertainment to Olympic votes. Tenor Luciano Pavarotti was part of Rome's team in the 1997 vote for the 2004 Games and Germany's World Cup-winning captain and coach Franz Beckenbauer went to Prague in 2003 to support Salzburg in their failed bid for the 2010 Winter Olympics. Yet, it was only after London announced that Beckham would be going to Singapore and New York confirmed the presence of boxing legend Muhammad Ali in their delegation that a new ruling was brought in to restrict the use of celebrities.

The IOC's ethics commission handed out more guidelines about the use of celebrities, saying prearranged photo-shoots involving stars and Singapore sports authorities and schools were banned before the vote.

The guideline seemed like an over-reaction. It was hard to see what a few pictures of Beckham had to do with stamping out corruption, the raison d'être of the IOC's ethics commission. In the end the guideline had little impact on the final campaigning of the five cities. In a carefully staged series of events, Beckham appeared at a British school in Singapore, met Tony Blair at a local sports event, appeared at a press conference and attended several functions.

London's focus on the promise of youth – and an East London boy turned global superstar – was a stark contrast to the Paris delegation which was dominated by middle-aged men in suits. London gave the impression they were looking forwards to a new era where Paris appeared to be looking to the past.

Beckham, himself, says getting a chance to be part of the historic meeting was something he could not have turned down. 'I was honoured when I got the phone call. At the time I had things planned and I turned around to Victoria and said, "I've just had this phone call and it's an incredible honour to be asked" so straight away I said yes.

'We had certain things planned with the family but I just thought: This is going to be part of history and to be a part of that will be special. London's a great place to host something like this, it's so passionate about all sport. As England captain I know that football fans are incredible, the passion and loyalty they show, and that's what London can bring.'

Did Beckham actually win any votes? That is hard to quantify exactly but his presence beside East London schoolchildren during London's final presentation was a powerful image for the members and the media. The odd autograph here and there would also have done no harm. IOC members may meet sports stars on a regular basis but they are also fathers, mothers and grandparents whose children and grandchildren would be very excited by a Beckham signature.

There is no doubt that Beckham enjoyed the whole experience, even if the attention got a bit scary at times. Lee explains: 'David wasn't due to stay for the announcement of the winning city but he became so excited by everything that he asked to stay on. He even wanted to come to the press conference after the result of the vote was announced. In fact, he snuck in at the back of the room before the conference started and sat down quietly, not knowing where we all were. It was only when I noticed that there was suddenly a media scrum of photographers on the other side of the room that I realised he was there.

'I was worried about it all getting out of hand and in the end I had to help get him out of the room, down into a corridor and into a secure area where the snappers couldn't go. The scrum was enveloping us but we escaped behind the security guards. That was when he coolly asked me if he and Victoria could come to the party in the evening. It was impressive. Even in the middle of all that madness, he kept his composure.

'My favourite Beckham moment was during a press conference when he was asked by a London TV reporter if his goal was to bring the Games to his "hood" (neighbourhood). David calmly replied, "Well, of course, I would like the Games to come back to my manor." David wasn't going to get drawn into using a word that was trendy but didn't come naturally to him. Even if the foreign reporters were a bit confused, it raised smiles around the room. There is no doubt that Beckham is well advised but I have learned that he does have a natural ability to understand the environment he is in. I never doubted the value of bringing him. He was a class act.'

While Beckham was doing most of his work for the bid in Singapore in front of hundreds of photographers, Tony Blair was securing crucial votes away from the limelight in private chats with IOC members over tea and biscuits at the Stamford Hotel.

Blair may be one of the most photogenic and eloquent Prime Ministers ever to enter Downing Street but it is widely recognised in political circles that he is an even better performer away from the cameras in one-on-one situations. One experienced newspaper editor says: 'However busy he is or, whatever his aides want him to do, Blair gives you his full attention. He sits there with a mug of tea in his hand and for those fifteen minutes or so, he gives you the impression that you are the most important person in the world. Maybe he is thinking of something else at times but you can never tell because he appears to be completely switched on to you.'

It was this side of the Prime Minister's character – not public sound bites or spin that sealed decisive votes in the final 72 hours before the IOC Session. The lobbying of Seb Coe, Keith Mills and Craig Reedie helped London 2012 arrive in Singapore feeling that they were in a good position to beat Paris. But the work of Tony and Cherie Blair in their luxury hotel suite gave London 2012 the extra push to get over the line ahead of the French.

The popular image of Olympic lobbying is of middle-aged men talking over gin and tonics in smoke-filled piano bars. But the Blairs did most of their entertaining in private over gallons of tea. On one level it may have been terribly British but it worked.

Although now and again the lobby of the Stamford Hotel would be full of bodyguards as the Blairs were swept from the lift to a car on the way to an official function in the city centre, the Prime Minister and his wife spent most of their hours in Singapore camped in their suites. The Blairs' Stamford Hotel was just a few steps away from the IOC's Raffles Hotel and the two main lobbies were connected by a corridor no longer than an Olympic 100-metres straight.

Away from the glare of the media, Reedie and Coe led around 25 IOC members along that 'home straight' and up to see the Prime Minister for 15-minute chats. Detailed profiles on the views of all IOC members had been put together by London 2012 staff. Before he was introduced to each member, Blair was given a note from Reedie containing key details on the delegate. It usually explained where the member was on the IOC hierarchy, where London 2012 felt he or she might vote and the issues which interested the member. Blair digested the briefs quickly. They allowed him to push the right buttons and avoid making any mistakes.

Reedie was impressed how quickly the Prime Minister could read a brief and act upon it. The Scot had witnessed the PM in action during meetings with IOC members at the Athens Games and during the celebrations of the BOA's centenary held at the House of Commons in May 2005. He describes his performance in one-on-one discussions as 'outstanding'.

In fact, the Prime Minister often did not even need to make a huge sales pitch for London. Sometimes it was just a matter of listening to the IOC member's views.

Blair explains: 'I was locked away in a room. It was extraordinary because I must have seen masses of people. They were coming in and going back at a great rate.

'Cherie came in too sometimes. Other times she would see the members herself. Sometimes people just wanted to come and say what they thought. Other times you were having to give a very strong pitch. Sometimes people would come in and say, "I have heard from the bid team about the Olympic bid, tell me about X and Y on the international scene" and I would give a sort of potted version of what was going on in the world.' Blair adds: 'I thoroughly enjoyed all those meetings. It was virtual back-to-back meetings, run with near-military precision. It was a long way to go. I also knew I couldn't stay for London's presentation or the voting because I had to host the G8 Heads of Government Summit in Scotland. London had assembled a fantastic team. We all had do what we could.'

These fifteen-minute tête-à-têtes helped to seal some crucial votes. Sometimes the conversations lasted for up to thirty minutes. It was a major logistical challenge to arrange them around the Prime Minister's schedule and the other one-to-ones. London 2012 ran six suites at the hotel and in total sixty-six individual meetings took place between IOC members and the London bid leadership. Keith Mills says the most important thing was to avoid members crossing in the corridor or waiting in a queue to see Blair. That would have stopped the meetings being special for the IOC members. So the timing of the meetings was crucial.

Mills says: 'We didn't want them lining up in the corridor. And when they went in to see the Prime Minister, we made sure that the conversations were relevant to that person. It wasn't just, "Nice to see you" and "What's the weather like?" We could not have done that without two years of homework on the IOC members.'

IOC members were both flattered and impressed that Blair had brought his office and staff to an IOC meeting for three days despite having to prepare to host a G8 summit with the leaders of the US, Japan, Germany, France, Italy, Canada and Russia in Scotland the same week, at which they were due to tackle major issues, including world poverty. By flying to the other side of the world with his wife and taking time to talk to IOC members individually, Blair had in one stroke quashed suggestions from London's rivals that the government was still not fully behind the bid.

In the whispering campaign that is an everyday part of Olympic bidding, London's opponents had put the idea into IOC members' minds that London still had only a 'virtual bid'. 'There were so many stadia to build,' they would say. 'Would the British government really be capable of building all those new stadia in East London? Look at Picketts Lock. What happened to the 2005 World Athletics Championships?'

Those tea and biscuits with the PM and his wife finally erased all of those doubts. It was not just the thirty or so undecided IOC members who were brought in to see Blair. Reedie and Coe made sure that even those they were 99 per cent sure were London supporters met the Prime Minister. It was important that every vote was 'nailed on'.

Cherie Blair recalls: 'I was convinced we were going to win. I knew we had the best bid. Tony was saying are you sure we can win this and I was saying "of course". You got the impression that the French were a bit "We're the French, here we are, let's have our Games". Confidence can be a good thing but it can be a vulnerability too sometimes. People had noticed we really wanted it and we had come from behind and we were definitely up there challenging. We had to give it absolutely everything. There was a relentless stream of people coming in to see us and we were able to talk to them about things you knew they were interested in. Occasionally there was a slip-up, like the time Tony started speaking to one of them thinking he was a javelin thrower but he turned out to be a gymnast. But that didn't happen very often.

'The Olympics is a family movement and talking to the wives was also quite important. A lot of the members appreciated our undivided attention. President Chirac came with his entourage but didn't really engage.'

London's belief in the importance of those meetings is backed by IOC members. Dick Pound, the former IOC vice-president from Canada, says: 'You couldn't have a better leader than Seb Coe. He's from central casting. But Blair made the difference.' Ireland's Pat Hickey, who is an influential figure among European members, was convinced within minutes of the announcement that Blair had played a substantial role. He said: 'The victory was down to Tony Blair. If he hadn't come to Singapore I'd say that six to eight votes would have been lost. The four votes that were in it in the final round were definitely down to him. Jacques Chirac came far too late.'

For most of the campaign the French President had been seen as a huge ally for Paris. Indeed he was perceived as the political leader who could swing the most votes. The 73-year-old was far more experienced in Olympic bidding than Blair, having been the Paris mayor when the French capital failed to win the 1992 Games in the mid-1980s. At the start of the campaign he knew far more IOC members personally.

There was also a widespread perception that, while Blair's support of George W. Bush in the Iraq war would lose London votes, Chirac's opposition to the conflict was definitely a vote winner.

IOC members are generally conservative in their politics and they like premiers with strong leadership qualities. Olympic Games organisers also need Prime Ministers and Presidents who can bang on the table and get things done if preparations are disrupted by construction delays, strikes or bureaucracy. It is not by chance that the IOC was led by Juan Antonio Samaranch for 21 years, a Spaniard who had a personal touch in private meetings but who firmly stamped his authority on the organisation in the 1980s and 1990s.

But by the time of the vote, the French President seemed to be losing his touch. He had just suffered a humiliating defeat at home in the referendum on the European Union constitution. Chirac's referendum failure contrasted sharply with Blair, who had just won a third term in office with a solid majority despite his unpopular decision to take Britain into the Iraq war. The showdown between Blair and Chirac was made even more interesting because of the political spats they had had in the previous two years. In the end the younger man got the political tactics just right and Chirac ended up looking like his best days of winning close votes were well behind him.

Chirac had travelled to Singapore with a huge logistical advantage. Because Paris had been drawn to make their presentation to the IOC first, it was possible for the French President to be involved in the presentation and make a speech to the IOC and then board a plane for the G8 summit. London would not make their presentation until after lunch and there was no way Blair could have taken part and then been in Gleneagles in Scotland in time to host the summit. But, while

Blair made up for his absence by getting to Singapore early, Chirac made possibly one of the biggest *faux pas* of his career by only turning up on the eve of the vote. It was a strange decision by a politician who knew that the IOC decision could have a huge impact not only on Paris and France but on his chances of staying in the presidency. A malaise was setting in France. The disappointment that spread through the streets of Paris when Rogge announced London's victory on 6 July will haunt Chirac forever.

In the two days before the vote, Paris 2012 officials could only sit in the café of the Stamford Hotel and watch in frustration as scores of IOC members were led up to see Blair. Jon Tibbs, the Paris PR adviser, claims that he tried to convince the French that they should get Chirac over to match Blair's initiative but his calls were not answered. The French knew they had left London 2012 an open goal and Blair had run into the penalty area and taken advantage of it with a cheeky grin on his face.

Worse still for the French, Chirac arrived in Singapore surrounded in controversy after reports that he had said that 'the only worse food than British food was Finnish' and that 'the only thing the British have done for Europe's agriculture is mad cow disease'. The remarks were made in private talks with German Chancellor Gerhard Schroeder and Russian President Vladimir Putin and were leaked to the French newspaper *Libération*.

Not only did the comments reduce Paris's hopes of getting the Finnish vote, they meant Chirac's arrival at the Raffles Hotel turned into an undignified scrum with one reporter asking: 'Do you like rosbif, Mr President?' Blair refused to be drawn into the row but it added extra spice to the VIP reception after the IOC Session's opening ceremony at the Esplanade Concert Hall when the Prime Minister and Chirac went head-to-head for votes in the final hours of the campaign.

The reception was an exclusive affair in an open-air balcony bar with Blair, Chirac and Hillary Clinton all in attendance. The Blairs had little time for drinks or canapés. They worked the room hard with Coe and Reedie introducing them to IOC members whom they had been unable to meet privately. Tessa Jowell and Richard Caborn were also speaking to as many IOC members as possible. London 2012 officials were mentally ticking off the members in their minds.

On one occasion, Jowell found herself talking to British journalists who had somehow managed to gatecrash the party in the slipstream of Hillary Clinton's entourage. It was not long before London 2012 lobbying strategist Andrew Craig was discreetly herding the culture secretary back to the IOC members like a trustworthy sheepdog. Jowell had been enjoying the little break from the lobbying but accepted she had gone astray and needed to return to the Olympic flock. 'Sorry, you guys don't have a vote,' Craig told the reporters.

Coe and Keith Mills always had a plan of action for every party. It was important that these rare occasions to lobby IOC members were used to the full. Tony Blair was very tired after racing across the world and was looking forward to a sleep on the plane that night on the way back to Britain. But the double Olympic champion squeezed every bit of entertaining he could out of the Prime Minister.

Blair says: 'It was an extraordinary cocktail party. I was very tired but Seb was very insistent. After an hour and a bit, I was flagging but he said, "You have got to stay and do some more." So we did.'

It was an unusual sight watching Blair, Chirac and Clinton in competition with each other for the attention of a hundred or so IOC members. But it was also indicative of the prestige in which the Olympics are held. Chirac kept away from the British Prime Minister for most of the party. Then, suddenly, the French President made his move to the Blairs and greeted the Prime Minister with a firm handshake and kissed Cherie on both cheeks. Chirac clearly liked the idea of a photo-call and his aides shepherded him towards Blair together with a few chosen photographers.

Tony Blair explains: 'I didn't mention his comments about British food. But I seem to remember that Cherie certainly did. As to the photograph, I didn't mind at all.'

The incident only lasted a few seconds but the French President needed to build bridges after his comments. The rapprochement, however, did not hide the fact that the Blairs had been working the room more effectively than either Chirac or Clinton. The

Blairs would have to leave the last day to Coe and his team but they had done everything they could in an intensive three days.

Mike Lee says: 'They are a powerful couple. They understand networking and they do have an impact on a room. Both have a nice touch with people and it certainly helps that the Prime Minister speaks French.

'I could see the level of the PM's engagement in the project. When he arrived in Singapore, Seb and I and the High Commissioner went out to the airport to meet him. His first words to us were "Let's go for it."

'Seb was a Tory peer but they had a very good relationship. He could see that Seb was the right man for the job. Seb was even allowed to address the Cabinet during the campaign. As he was about to talk to the meeting at Number 10, the Prime Minister joked: "I bet you never thought you would be sitting here." Seb looked around the table at the Labour Cabinet and replied: "Certainly not in this company."'

The public relations campaign for the Blairs during the Olympic bid was handled in a completely different way to anything else the Prime Minister has done. Cherie Blair often struggles to get good publicity in the domestic media so she did no briefings or press conferences with the British media. In fact, at the request of Mike Lee, Number 10 turned its usual PR strategy upside down in the last months of the bid and put the international media ahead of British newspapers and TV.

The international agencies like Reuters, Associated Press and Agence France Presse and global TV stations like CNN are regarded as 'no-votes' outlets during a general election, but suddenly they were the key players in this campaign because their reports could reach IOC members across the world. The IOC correspondents of Reuters, AP and AFP were invited to Number 10 for an exclusive briefing, as was Ed Hula, the American who runs the influential *Around the Rings* newsletter and website.

This access to the Blairs was not provided to the national press. In Singapore, Blair even held a press conference where only international journalists could ask the questions. The likes of Sky's Adam Boulton and other political heavyweight journalists were forced to sit on their hands, a rare experience for reporters used to posing the first questions to the Prime Minister, as he responded to the probing of the Olympic media pack.

As a former Labour spin doctor, Mike Lee was respected by the Number 10 press office. He says: 'The Prime Minister realised this was an election campaign which required very different tactics to a general election. The Number 10 press office trusted us when we said people like Ed Hula were really important.'

'Political support was a real issue for us after Picketts Lock. We needed to address it. Blair was essential to the victory. He made that final push in Singapore with those one-on-ones. He was also essential to our final media drive. Nobody should underestimate the power of the Blair brand internationally, it made a big difference at a crucial time.'

Lee describes Beckham and Blair as the two great 'British brands'. He is convinced that without them, London would not have won. 'They are both skilled at handling the mass media. They know what it takes and were happy to do what was necessary. But at the same time they were fantastic team players. We couldn't have asked for any more.'

11. 'WE'VE WON!'

Tony and Cherie Blair were already on board their plane to Scotland by the time Mike Lee returned to the Raffles Hotel after the IOC Session's opening ceremony. After the cocktail party where the Blairs had been working the room in competition with Jacques Chirac and Hillary Clinton, the Prime Minister made one last push for votes during private drinks with IOC members from the Commonwealth in his hotel suite. Most of the members were nailed-on London voters but, as a seasoned political campaigner, Blair knew the importance of making sure there were no problems at all with the core vote.

As a politician, Blair had relished the last-minute lobbying, feeling at home in the hectic world of electioneering. But the Prime Minister and his wife were exhausted after a long day. Before being driven to the airport to fly back to Britain for the G8 summit, Blair took off his tie, jacket and shoes and enjoyed a beer with Cherie, Seb Coe and Keith Mills in his hotel suite. It was past 11 p.m.

Mills explains: 'We sat around on the sofas with ties and shoes off and relaxed for a moment. Given the fact he was getting ready for the G8 summit the Prime Minister put in a huge effort. We could not have asked for more. But as we sat there he joked, "I thought I worked hard but you guys are animals."'

Despite their fatigue, Tony and Cherie Blair left Singapore feeling elated. Cherie Blair recalls: 'On the plane we did feel really excited. I remember Tony definitely saying that he was glad he went and that it had made a difference.'

Lee had missed the cocktail party at the Esplanade Theatre. The communications chief had been doing a series of interviews for the media in Britain which, because of the time difference, was still hungry for news about the campaign for the early-evening news bulletins. He then held a meeting with his staff at the Carlton Hotel to discuss the following day's media plans.

As he walked from the Carlton to the Raffles Hotel around midnight, Lee could hardly believe there were less than 24 hours remaining in the 2012 campaign. He had spent most of the previous two years eating, drinking and sleeping the bid. All of those efforts had been focused on 6 July. Now the day of judgement was about to arrive.

It was another warm night in Singapore and Lee took his time to walk the two blocks. He wondered for a moment how he would be feeling at the same time the next day.

There are few jobs or organisations where everything is judged by the events of just one day. But after 7.46 p.m. on 6 July, Lee knew that the staff of four of the bidding teams would be looking for a new job. He could easily be among them. General elections are different in that respect – political parties still exist after polling day and, although some staff change, many people carry on to fight another day. Olympic bidding is a cruel, risky business. It's a gruelling, emotional ride that ends in ecstasy or bitter disappointment. There are no prizes for finishing second. Nobody remembers the city that just failed to get the Olympics and Lee knew defeat would be hard to swallow, however close the result.

But unlike the eve of a general election when all the campaigning is done, the party political broadcasts have gone out and the politicians spend polling day just waiting for the result, the London 2012 team still had the chance to woo votes in the final presentation, just hours before the decision.

Each city would make a 45-minute presentation to the IOC members throughout the day before the vote in the early evening. In the past a city has rarely been awarded the Games on the strength of a presentation alone. But all the cities knew that in such a tight race, a good presentation only needs to attract a couple of extra votes to change the outcome.

Lee was pleased that very few details of the theme of London's presentation had leaked out, apart from the 'official' authorised teasers. He was confident that it would come as a surprise to IOC members. But would London 2012's vision for the Games be powerful enough to persuade them to vote Britain's way? Or would the emotional pull of Paris bidding for a third time win the day? Would all the hard months of lobbying by Sebastian Coe, Craig Reedie, Keith Mills and Tony Blair be enough to pull it off? Would the successful communications campaign really affect the vote? These questions and doubts flooded through Lee's mind over those couple of blocks.

He comforted himself with the thought that rarely has the favourite in an Olympic bidding race actually won the vote, especially in the Summer Games. Beijing's victory in the 2008 race was a rare exception because the political pull of taking the Games to China for the first time was so powerful. The Chinese capital had dominated the campaign from start to finish. But Rome had been the favourite to win the 2004 Games for most of the campaign before Athens won the vote in 1997. Beijing had been expected to win the 2000 Games but Sydney snatched victory at the last minute in the tightest vote in Olympic history. Paris 2012 officials also knew their bidding history and it was well known that the French were uncomfortable with the favourite tag.

Lee could not go to sleep with all these thoughts buzzing around his head. He knew 6 July would be a long day but he made for the Ink Club bar on the ground floor of the Raffles Hotel. He says: 'I wanted to test the water with some of the serious international Olympic journalists. We had finished the last three days of the communications campaign and I wanted to get a feeling about where London was on the eve of the vote, as far as the media was concerned.

'And the Ink Club that night turned out to be an exhilarating moment. For the first time, I started to get the feeling that victory might be ours. What was striking was that some of the seasoned IOC-beat journalists were saying London could do it. Ed Hula from *Around the Rings* told me he thought London had won it. Not many of the British media were predicting a London victory apart from Adrian Warner of the *Evening Standard* and Duncan Mackay of the *Guardian*. But Adrian and Duncan were reporters who knew IOC members well and talked to them on a regular basis. I respected what they had to say.

'These predictions would have been unthinkable twelve months before. Those conversations in the bar gave me a huge boost. I left the Ink Club with a clear head but I have to admit my nerves were starting to jangle more than ever before. Before I had always hoped we could win. Suddenly, I was starting to feel it was now on.'

Few people from the bid cities slept well that night. All the bidding teams were up early the next morning and the Raffles Hotel lobby was buzzing at breakfast time. The Paris 2012 team appeared jovial and confident as they tucked into a continental breakfast in the ground-floor restaurant. The French needed to be on top of their form especially early because Paris were to open the presentations in the morning. London was the fourth city to make a presentation and had the disadvantage of the slot just after lunch. Unlike the French, Coe and his team also had a whole morning to think about their speeches. The danger was they could get too nervous.

Lee was up at 7 a.m. He was determined to keep a close eye on what London's rivals were saying and doing. There had been various rumours that Paris had an exceptional presentation. Lee got up early for another reason: 'It was a big day in my professional life. Waking up I felt what a footballer must feel on the morning of a World Cup final: plenty of nerves but huge excitement about the hours ahead. I had a feeling it was going to be a special day and I felt that the London bid was in the best possible shape. But I knew we had to get the presentation right. My first job was to feed some of the key elements of our presentation to journalists I could trust who were on tight deadlines. They agreed to confidentiality and by knowing early they had more time to prepare their stories and scripts in advance. Then we had to start watching the other presentations, starting with the French.'

Most of the London 2012 team moved into the Stamford Hotel suites vacated by Tony and Cherie Blair where many of the one-on-one chats with IOC members had taken place. The Blairs' suites became London 2012's 'Mission Control' for the day. A live television feed of the IOC Session was piped into a nearby room, where the technical team, led by marketing chief David Magliano, analysed the other bids' presentations and the questions IOC members asked after the presentations.

Lee explains: 'We had to know what the potential questions might be for London and to draft our answers in advance. Seb would be answering most of the questions but we were also determined to make sure Ken Livingstone did not go off message in his answers. Ken is a confident speaker and he often improvises. If there were questions about transport there might be the danger that he would talk about decades of under-investment before he took office. Whilst that might be OK for a domestic audience, we didn't want him talking about under investment to the IOC. Ken made clear he was happy to leave all questions to Seb if that helped us win.'

But as the team sat down to listen to the Paris presentation, one key figure from London 2012 was missing from Mission Control – Seb Coe. It was decided that the London 2012 chairman should not get too caught up in the presentations of the other bids. Just like in his running days, Coe concentrated on his own performance rather than worrying about what his rivals were doing. His job was to perfect his speech and be ready to answer any questions. His job was also to stay relaxed so that he could focus all of his energy on London's presentation.

The double Olympic champion occasionally popped his head into Mission Control. But Coe spent the morning reading through his speech, shopping and relaxing in his room listening to modern jazz on a CD player he had brought to Singapore. So when President Jacques Chirac was addressing the Session and most of London 2012's officials were on the edge of their seats watching film director Luc Besson's video and analysing its potential impact, Coe was strolling through the shopping centre near the Raffles Hotel complex thinking about what presents he should buy for his four children.

Coe's PA Susie Black has known the Olympic champion since the days when they both worked for former Conservative party leader William Hague and has a good sense of the character of the man. But she admits it was a strange moment walking with him through the shopping centre while the rest of the delegation – and most of the Olympic world – were engrossed in the Paris presentation. Susie says: 'All morning he refused to watch the presentations. I remember walking around the shopping centre, trying to snatch a glimpse of the French film on the TV sets around the mall. But Seb was just waltzing around thinking about the kids' presents. It really was surreal. But he likes wandering around like that. He had also been worried that he wouldn't have time to get the presents later. I think he just doesn't like to be surrounded by lots of people.'

Coe admits his reluctance to watch his rivals dates back to his running days: 'I never watched the athletes I was running against before a race. I never found I could learn very much. My coach always sat through the heats and made some notes about what they did. In the end, I always left my tactics flexible. I was not that interested in watching the other presentations in Singapore. It was too late to make any alterations to our presentation, anyway. We knew pretty much what was going to be said by the others after two years of campaigning. I did sense, however, that the level of questioning would be high because the race was so close. In the middle of the shopping, I did break off to the listen to the Question and Answer session with Paris on one of the screens.'

Coe returned to his hotel suite after the shopping. Mike Lee and Keith Mills occasionally popped in to discuss the feedback from the other presentations and rehearse possible questions he could face. But for most of the time, Coe prepared for the biggest moment of his public life away from the track alone in his room. Now and again he would look through his speech but for most of the morning he just relaxed listening to the music of the jazz pianist Jimmy Rowles. The American musician was best known for being the accompanist to the great singers Billie Holiday, Peggy Lee and Ella Fitzgerald.

Now, nearly ten years after his death, Rowles was providing the inspiration for the words of Seb Coe.

Lee, meanwhile, was worrying about Paris for him. There had been rumours that the French had a major surprise in their presentation. It had been rumoured that the Luc Besson film was going to be such a big part of the presentation that the French must have something up their sleeves which could be as dramatic as London's vision. The London 2012 team sat nervously in front of the TV in Mission Control. Lee poured himself a cup of coffee, nibbled nervously at a biscuit and prayed that the French were not about to steal London's thunder.

He need not have worried. Like a defensive football team protecting a 1–0 lead, the Paris bid played safe again. The French produced a solid presentation but it failed to take off. The Besson work was clever, showing off the flavour of the French capital with traditional accordion music in the background. The film used computer graphics of the five Olympic rings in front of the Eiffel Tower particularly well. But it was lengthy and there was a huge flaw in the overall presentation: it lacked real emotion – it said nothing about the future. Onstage were the usual white men in dark suits. No black athletes, who play such an important part in France's sporting life, were given the opportunity to make a speech. Astonishingly, women did not play a major role in the presentation either. It was as if the French had decided that the best way to appeal to a body made up largely of men over sixty was to put men in suits in front of them and remind them of how wonderful the French were at food, wine and sport.

It might have worked a decade ago. But the IOC's membership was changing, with more former athletes coming into the organisation. Paris Mayor Bertrand Delanoe and Chirac made solid but uninspired speeches. Delanoe stressed the huge support in France for the Games to come to Paris. But Chirac lacked the sparkle he had shown on previous occasions in front of the IOC.

Lee says: 'I have to say my verdict on the Paris presentation was that it was a bit flat. I think the video was completely overdone and the bid was delivered largely by political figures. There was also nothing new in it. It all felt a bit like a French tourist information advert and then there was no emotional connection in the speeches. I do think they did a great job with the Olympic rings but there was nothing in the whole thing to cause us any anxiety.'

With the Paris presentation out of the way, Lee sat down in Mission Control to watch the efforts of New York and Moscow. There were few surprises.

The American presentation was full of razzmatazz. It stressed the vibrancy of a 'city that never sleeps' and it was not long before the strains of Frank Sinatra's famous number 'New York, New York' filled the ballroom. Muhammad Ali, who had famously carried the Olympic flame at the 1996 Atlanta Olympics in hands shaking violently because of Parkinson's disease, was introduced to the IOC members to prolonged applause. Alluding to the September 11 attacks on the Twin Towers, Mayor Michael Bloomberg made an emotional speech. He said: 'New Yorkers asked ourselves "Can we recover, will we rebuild?" Without hesitation, New Yorkers stood up and said yes. This spirit will be given to your Games. New Yorkers never give up – not now, not ever.'

Moscow pulled off a clever stunt with Russian President Vladimir Putin speaking English in public for the first time on a video. But his ideas were hardly revolutionary. He said: 'The Games, if held in Moscow, would be the best in the history of the Olympic movement. Moscow is a meeting place of cultures. This is a time when our country, having come through deep economic transformations, has ever-increasing possibilities.'

Mike Lee and David Magliano listened carefully but their minds were now beginning to focus on London's chance to shine after lunch. The team was ready. Every word had been rehearsed time after time in Sentosa and in Singapore. Even the body language of every key figure on the stage had been analysed and perfected in the final rehearsals.

Lee says: 'We rehearsed the presentation in the ballroom in the final two days before the vote. We worked on absolutely everything. We studied the body language of every member of the delegation on the platform. It was important that everybody sat in a positive way, nobody slumped in their chair or looked tired or bored. It was decided that, when a speaker was at the lectern, the eleven other people sitting on the stage would look towards him or her. Nobody was allowed to look at the films we would show on the monitors facing them because it looked negative to look downwards. Everybody had to turn to look at the large screens on stage. That was much more positive. Keith Mills and Ken Livingstone needed the odd reminder in rehearsals.

'The rehearsals in the Raffles ballroom were behind closed doors with only a select number of IOC people allowed to observe them. For the first time you could really feel how dramatic our presentation was going to be. But I knew it was no good scoring loads of goals in training if you fail to deliver during the match. We knew we had to get it right on the day.'

As the IOC members tucked into their lunch after the first three presentations, the London 2012 team gathered all dressed in their summery beige suits and blue shirts, the official outfit. The men wore a multicoloured striped tie. The London delegation had agreed to assemble around an hour before the presentation was due to start so that everybody had plenty of time to get ready. When the team came together, however, Susie Black noticed that Seb Coe was still missing, fifteen minutes after the deadline. As she made her way back to Coe's suite to check he was OK, the two mobiles she was carrying started to ring, almost in panic. The producers of the presentation were clearly getting nervous that he had yet to turn up.

She explains: 'Some of them were starting to have kittens. The phones started going off. After about twenty minutes, I went up to his room. I wasn't sure whether to go in but I decided I had to. When I put my head around the door, I saw Seb still lying on the bed listening to jazz at top volume. He hadn't even got into his official bid suit yet. He didn't see me come in. I had to prod him. I said something like "I think we need to get going now" and I got out of the way so he could get dressed. It didn't take long. Seb had refused to have any make-up they were offering and he didn't like anyone doing anything to his hair. About twenty minutes before the start of the presentation, he was ready to go. But when I looked at him, he was yawning. He said: "Don't worry, that's good. It means the adrenaline is flowing."

'Then I found out that he has one superstition from his running days. Whenever he left a hotel room – or a room in the athletes' village – he never went back to it before a race. He still does that on big occasions. So we stood there checking we had everything several times – key, speech, reading glasses – and then we made our way to the rest of the delegation. When he came out of the lift and to the assembly point, everybody stood up. He was clearly moved by that. Then almost immediately the delegation was called into the room. Seb wasn't being irresponsible or anything like that turning up later than the others. He just doesn't like hanging around waiting for something.'

Coe says he used exactly the same tactics when he was racing. He always went to the warm-up area or the call-up area in the stadium at the last minute. He explains: 'I never went to a call-up area earlier than I needed to when I was running. I have never liked hanging around waiting for something to happen. And the Singapore presentation was one of the top three public moments in my life, up there with the Moscow and Los Angeles Olympics. There was also nothing to say to the team then. We all knew that we needed to give Oscar-winning performances. I didn't need to say that to any of the team. They knew it.'

Once Coe had arrived, London prepared to unveil the first part of its powerful image about the 2012 Games being for the children of the next generation. To the surprise of many IOC members and the assembled media, more than a third of London's 100-strong delegation was made up of children from East London schools, 30 kids from 28 different ethnic backgrounds. They had been brought to Singapore as an embodiment of London's multicultural society. The contingent also included Amber Charles, the fourteen-year-old basketball player from East London who had delivered London's bid book in November 2004. Each of the children went into the ballroom hand in hand with other sporting ambassadors such as David Beckham and Steve Redgrave. Amber Charles joined Seb Coe and London 2012's leading figures on the platform while the rest of the children sat in the audience with Beckham and the other sports stars.

It was the most dramatic entry of a candidate city in the history of Olympic bidding.

The idea of filling London's delegation with children had first been suggested by Roger Jackson, a Canadian consultant who had been involved in Vancouver's successful bid for the 2010 Winter Games. Mike Lee remembers the moment very well. Keith Mills was having a meeting with Jackson in his office at Canary Wharf the previous May when he called Lee into his office. 'Keith told me to come in and bring an extra seat. Then when I was sitting comfortably, he said: "Roger has just come up with a great idea. Why don't we fill up the whole of our London 2012 delegation – apart from the main speakers of course – with a hundred children from east London?" I said I loved the idea but was not sure that we could do it quite on that scale. I conveyed the proposal to Seb and David Magliano who both agreed it could be a great symbol. But I have to say it did not have the full support of everybody in the bid. Tessa Jowell, Craig Reedie, Seb, Keith, myself and Magliano all saw the potential of the children as a strong message of what London's bid was all about. My senior colleagues in the communications team were totally behind it. But there was opposition from some who thought it might be regarded as a cheap stunt and backfire on us because the children might not behave correctly. But we pushed it through. After several, at times heated, meetings and conference calls a compromise was finally reached where it was decided to go ahead with the kids representing around a third of the delegation.'

London was keen not only to show IOC members this special image. It wanted the world watching on TV to see it clearly too. During the rehearsals, Sara Donaldson of Live, who oversaw the production of the presentation, worked with the IOC's television producers and directors to make sure a good 'cut-away' shot would be shown of the contingent when they were mentioned in Coe's speech. Like the lobbying campaign, the presentation was run like a military operation.

Lee explains: 'Everything had to be planned on a micro level, from who would be sitting on the stage with Seb to how we would walk into the room. When they walked in, everybody looked fantastic in their uniforms. The mood was buoyant. The rest of the bid staff, who were not going into the room, clapped us in. It really was like going out for an Olympic final. And everybody was up for it.'

The London delegation was welcomed into the room by IOC President Jacques Rogge and then the curtain went up on the show. London followed protocol by starting with speeches by Britain's IOC members, the Princess Royal and Craig Reedie. Princess Anne's short speech included a message of support for the London bid from the Queen. Then Craig Reedie sent the first poignant message to IOC members by opening his speech in French. Reedie usually addresses the IOC in English. By beginning in French, he not only startled his IOC colleagues but he also made a serious point about the British bid. London was saying to the members: 'Listen. Forget all the old stereotypes about the British and their reluctance to speak foreign languages. We are coming this time with a different bid from a different Britain with an international outlook.' The point was to be stressed again later in the presentation in a video from Tony Blair in which the Prime Minister also begins in faultless French.

There was a hint of nerves in Reedie's voice but he spoke clearly and with emotion. He told the Session that British teams had participated at all of the Olympic Games since 1896 and had also been the 'cradle' for the Paralympic movement.

Then, without mentioning Paris, the Scot quickly addressed France's greatest weapon in the 2012 race – the fact that Paris was bidding for a third time. Reedie had mentioned in previous presentations during the campaign how Britain had listened to IOC members after the three failed bids from Birmingham and Manchester and answered their calls for London to be brought to the table. It was always hard for a regional city to win a bidding race and only London had a real chance of winning. Now he told the Session: 'No other country has made a greater effort than Britain to host the Summer Games. This is our fourth bid in twenty years. We have learned from each of the three previous bids. We understand the recipe for magical Games.' Like a sophisticated party political broadcast, London wasted no time in taking on the strength of its main rival in a discreet but clear way.

Then Reedie introduced London's special vision for the 2012 Olympics. He said: 'If you grant the Games to London, you will place in our hands the Olympic spirit. We will guard that spirit, we will cherish it and we will proudly hand it on to young people like those in this film.' Then the first part of the 'Inspiration' film was played to the IOC members. It began with a shot of a black sprinter waiting to start the Olympic 100 metres final. In a deep voice, the commentator said: 'To make an Olympic champion it takes eight Olympic finalists. To make Olympic finalists, it takes 80 Olympians. To make Olympians it takes 202 national champions. To make national champions it takes thousands of athletes. To make athletes, it takes millions of children around the world to be inspired to choose sport.'

The film then moved to a scene in a poor street in Africa with children wasting time in the street throwing stones at a can. A police car rolls by with an officer taking a close look at the children through his side window. Then one of the young boys, no older than 10, catches sight of the 100 metres final from London on a TV in a bar. He turns away from his stone throwing and watches the screen as the commentator shouts: 'It's Nigeria's Tony Neery, the Olympic 100 metres champion.'

The film was then stopped and, right on cue, Seb Coe began the most emotional speech of his life. He said: 'Mr President, members of the IOC, to make an Olympic champion takes millions of young people around the world to be inspired to choose Olympic sport. In the past London and the Olympic movement have come together to face serious challenges.' Coe went on to explain how London stepped in to stage the Games in difficult days in 1908 when it delivered the first purpose-built Olympic stadium and in 1948 in rationing after the Second World War when the first volunteer programme was introduced. Then he added: 'Today London is ready to join you to face a new challenge, to provide an enduring sporting legacy. Today's challenge is tough and more complex. We can no longer take it for granted that young people will choose sport. Some may lack the facilities or the coaches or the role models. Others, in an age of 24-hour entertainment and instant fame, may simply lack the desire. We are determined that London's Games will address this challenge. London's vision is to reach people all around the world to connect them with the inspirational power of the Games so that they are inspired to choose sport.' It was as if a full orchestra had started playing the '1812' Overture at full volume in the ballroom. Every IOC member was awake and alert. Coe had grabbed the attention of the members with a theme which they all recognised as a serious problem around the world. Unlike the other presentations, London had not started its show with spectacular shots of its city. This was no tourist presentation.

More importantly, instead of holding out hands begging to be given the Games, London 2012 was offering the IOC a strong hand to get out of an increasingly worrying situation. It was an approach which was so dramatically different to bidding cities in the past that it both startled and fascinated the IOC members. They wanted to hear what was coming next.

Coe then introduced Amber Charles and the thirty children from East London sitting in the delegation in the main auditorium. They all waved to the camera on cue and that shot of the children was broadcast both on the big screen in the room for the IOC members to see and around the world. Coe continued: 'Why are so many here taking the place of businessmen and politicians? It's because we are serious about inspiring young people. Each is from East London, a community that will be touched by the Games. They are a multicultural mix of two hundred nations representing the youth of the world, families from every continent, practising every religion. What unites them is their love of sport, London and the dream of bringing the Olympic Games to our city.'

Coe then moved on to the technical aspects of the bid, cleverly thanking IOC members for their input in helping London to formulate its ideas. Keeping a humble approach was crucial to the whole of the presentation. Given that London's vision focused on a serious problem in the Olympic world, it was important that Coe was not seen to preach or show any hint of arrogance. Coe explains: 'From early on, we knew we had to provide a challenge *and* a solution. It could not be provocative. It had to be counselling, rather than lecturing.'

Coe's speech was split up into several parts and he introduced several other speakers. The members were shown a video of London's most spectacular venues – Wembley, Wimbledon and Horse Guards Parade. They were told that London would provide the most compact Games ever where athletes could walk from their rooms in the Olympic village to many of the venues.

Then Denise Lewis walked confidently up to the lectern. Her presence as a black female athlete at the heart of the London presentation team contrasted sharply with a Paris show dominated by white men in suits. Lewis is one of Britain's most famous athletes, having won a bronze medal in the heptathlon at the 1996 Atlanta Games and then gold at the 2000 Sydney Games. She is also one of the sport's most glamorous figures. Her fame and talents go way beyond athletics, having finished runner-up in the BBC's *Strictly Coming Dancing* competition in 2004. Lewis was a confident and photogenic performer.

As a member of London 2012's athletes' commission, she told the IOC that the most important thing for Olympic competitors was to have an athletes' village that was conveniently placed for the venues. By putting the village at the heart of the Olympic Park within walking distance of the main stadium, London's plans were perfect, she said. 'In London athletes will compete and not commute. It makes all the difference to be as close to the action as possible. When a fraction of a second or a fraction of a centimetre can be the difference between winning or losing and can change your life, you appreciate it when the small details have been thought out many years before.' She finished her speech with a link to a video about the 'Magic of London'.

The film was the only time that London played its tourist card. Most of the members had visited the city many times and they did not need to sit through endless videos about the Houses of Parliament, Big Ben and the Tower of London. The video was short, sharp and to the point. It was divided into headlines: 'A Royal Welcome' with shots of the Queen and Horse Guards Parade; 'A Festival of Culture' with pictures of Elton John and orchestras performing; 'A Home for Every Nation' with shots of children of all races and religions; and 'A Passion for Sport' with action involving the Wimbledon tennis championships, Arsenal, David Beckham, Denise Lewis and

Paula Radcliffe. The film finished with footage of Kelly Holmes winning her 800 metres gold medal in Athens and with the message: 'London, where magic happens'.

By the time the film had finished, Ken Livingstone was standing at the lectern. He began: 'That film gave you a flavour of our city. London is a city which welcomes the world with open arms but also with an open mind.' There was a definite croak in the London mayor's voice. Behind his public image as a controversial and outspoken character, Livingstone is a man with a soft centre. He is immensely proud of the capital. Although he has never been an avid sports fan, Livingstone got emotionally involved in the bid because of its potential to change the face of a place he loved.

Lee explains: 'Ken cried in every rehearsal he was at. Ken simply loves London. The "Inspiration" and "Magic of London" films got to him particularly. During one rehearsal he came up to me and said: "I'm just crying because those films really moved me."' The mayor was to face far more challenging and emotional times in the next 24 hours in Singapore. But on 6 July his mind was focused on getting over his message about London's strength as a magnet for young people from all over the world. He pointed to the successful Live 8 concerts which had just taken place in the city before the Singapore meeting. He said: 'As the organisers of the Live 8 concerts will tell you, if you wish to mobilise the youth of the world, start in London.'

London 2012 was clever in the way it put over its messages in simple digestible bites. The speeches were not too long and every speaker had a message which was easy for the IOC members to understand. They were being rolled out well: Coe on the vision of inspiring children to take up sport; Denise Lewis on a bid designed for athletes; Livingstone on a city which was a magnet for the youth of the world.

Then London 2012 pulled off another coup. Tony Blair appeared in a video message recorded at Downing Street in which the Prime Minister began in perfect French. He told the members that he had been honoured to meet many of them in Singapore and stressed that the bid had the support of both the government and the nation. He brought a message of support from Nelson Mandela, quoting the former South African President saying that he could not think of a better place than London to unite the world. Blair said: 'As a leader in government or sport, we have a duty to reach beyond our own time and borders, to have a vision which serves those who come after us. Our vision is for millions more young people in Britain and around the world to participate in sport and improve lives. London has the power to make that happen. It is a city with a voice which talks to young people.'

Tessa Jowell followed the video by telling the IOC how the Olympic Park and an Olympic Institute in Stratford would provide training, competition and research facilities for sportsmen and women from around the world for generations to come. London 2012 was determined that no white elephants would be left behind after the Games. Jowell stressed that the Games would help create the biggest urban park in Europe for two hundred years.

The main technical elements of the bid had now been delivered. The presentation was building towards an emotional climax. The last part of the 'Inspiration' film was played with the young runner, gymnast, cyclist and swimmer all finally developing into Olympic athletes.

Then Coe began the final part of his script. He had rehearsed and rewritten the words of this part of the speech so many times. Every sentence had been analysed and sub-edited so that it struck the right code. Even the first six words were significant. Coe began: 'Mr President. Mr Honorary Life President.' The London 2012 bid chairman made a special point of mentioning Juan Antonio Samaranch with whom he had enjoyed a special relationship since his running days. Relations with Madrid had been good. It was important to remind members who were likely to vote for Madrid about that strong Anglo-Spanish bond. Once Madrid was out of the contest, if the votes went as the team had predicted, they could have the confidence to vote for London.

Like an actor building up to a crucial monologue, Coe then talked of how he had been led into a school hall in Sheffield at the age of twelve to watch pictures from the Mexico City Olympics in 1968 on a black-and-white TV set. On the grainy pictures, local athlete John Sherwood was winning a bronze medal in the 400 metres hurdles behind an inspirational David Hemery. Sherwood's wife Sheila narrowly missed out on winning a gold medal in the long jump. Coe said: 'That day a window to a new world opened for me. By the time I was back in my classroom, I knew what I wanted to be and what I wanted to do. The following week I stood in line for hours at my local track to catch a glimpse of the medals the Sherwoods had brought home. It didn't stop there. Two days later, I joined their club. Two years later, Sheila gave me my first pair of racing spikes. Thirty-five years on, I stand before you with those memories still fresh, still inspired by this great movement. My journey here to Singapore started in that school hall and continues today in wonder and in gratitude. Gratitude that those flickering images drew me to a life in that most potent celebration of humanity, Olympic sport. And that gratitude drives me and my team to do whatever we can to inspire young people to choose sport, whoever they are, wherever they live and whatever they believe.

'Today that task is so much harder. Today's children live in a world of conflicting messages and competing distractions. Their landscape is cluttered. Their path to Olympic sport is often obscured. But it's a world we must understand and must respond to. My heroes were Olympians. My children's heroes change by the month. And they are the lucky ones. Millions more face the obstacle of limited resources and the resulting lack of guiding role models. In my travels over the last two years, speaking with many of you, I've had many conversations about how we meet this challenge. And I've been reassured and I've been uplifted we share a common goal for the future of sport. No group of leaders does more than you to engage the hearts and minds of young people. But every year the challenge of bringing them to Olympic sport becomes tougher. The choice of host city is the most powerful means you have to meet this challenge. But it takes more than seventeen days of superb Olympic competition. It takes a broader vision. And the global voice to communicate that vision over the full four years of the Olympiad.

'Today in Britain's fourth bid in recent years we offer London's vision of inspiration and legacy. Choose London today and you send a clear message to the youth of the world: more than ever, the Olympic Games are for you. Mr President, members of the IOC, some might say that your decision today is between five similar bids. That would be to undervalue the opportunity before you. In the past you have made bold decisions. Decisions which have taken the movement forwards in new and exciting directions. Your decision today is critical. It is a decision about which bid offers the vision and sporting legacy to best promote the Olympic cause. It is a decision about which city will help us show a new generation why sport matters. In a world of many distractions, why Olympic sport matters. And in the twenty-first century why the Olympic ideals still matter so much.

'On behalf of the youth of today, the athletes of tomorrow and the Olympians of the future, we humbly submit the bid of London 2012.'

Applause echoed around the room. Coe had delivered the most powerful speech in the history of Olympic bidding. The message had been delivered in the perfect tone. Every word of the last sentence of Coe's speech had been carefully chosen. London 2012 was not preaching to the IOC. It was 'humbly' offering to help solve one of the biggest problems facing global sport. The hours and hours of rehearsals had been all worthwhile.

Mike Lee had looked nervously around the room from his delegation seat in the front row of the auditorium during most of the speech. He had direct eye contact with the members of the evaluation commission who had visited London in the previous February. David Beckham and the group of children from East London were nearby. By the time Coe delivered his final words, Lee's nerves had turned to excitement.

He explains: 'Everything felt right. I felt there was a real buzz in the room and a strong resonance. I could see people were really gripped by the presentation. People clearly felt very moved. I had been in the thick of it and I felt moved. In some ways what we were doing was very risky. We were laying down a challenge. We were saying the Olympic movement had a problem, an ageing demographic and fewer young people taking up sport. If we had pointed out this problem in the wrong way, the whole idea might have backfired. We could have been seen as arrogant. The last thing a bidding city should do is give a sermon to the IOC. But we presented it as a challenge which London wanted to tackle together with the IOC. It was less of a sermon and more of a prayer and it suggested a partnership for the future. Seb's speech was crucial in this. The reason I felt so good was that Seb got the tone absolutely right.

'The key point was that our narrative was much more about the Olympic movement than about London – we were creating the terms for an historic choice. We also turned potential negatives into positives by emphasising legacy and London as a global media centre, capable of reaching the whole world and helping the IOC transmit the call for more young people to take up sport. We faced no difficult questions from the IOC directly afterwards. There was a question about the sailing being two and a half hours away in Weymouth and we explained there was an on-site athletes village nearby. When the team got together outside of the ballroom afterwards, there was a real sense of euphoria. We all felt the presentation could not have gone better. I said to Seb: "That was perfect." He replied simply: "Yes, it felt good."'

The press conference that followed was still carrying some of the energy and emotion and the London team expressed their belief that nothing more could have been done. Afterwards, as most of the presentation team returned to the Carlton Hotel, they met up with the rest of the London 2012 delegation who had been watching the Session on a live TV feed. Mission Control was still in operation in Tony Blair's former hotel suite but the *raison d'être* of the group was now over, given that London had coped easily with the IOC's post-presentation questions.

A handful of London 2012 people watched the final presentation from Madrid, however. It focused on the idea of a Madrid Games promoting peace and bringing nations together. The IOC was told that Spain was on good terms with all countries in the world. But the Spanish videos were predictable, featuring flamenco dancing, beaches, city life and sport over a soundtrack of rousing guitar music. Madrid had not brought a big idea to Singapore like London.

Coe returned to his hotel room for a shower while Lee began to prepare for the best- and worst-case scenarios in the couple of hours that followed. What would London 2012's leaders say if they lost the vote? What would they say if they won? What would they say if everything went wrong and the city went out in the first round of voting?

Before the vote, Tessa Jowell, British Olympic Association Chief Executive Simon Clegg and Ken Livingstone sat down with Lee to run through the various scenarios. Preparation is obviously a key part of any communications campaign. Being ready for all eventualities is crucial. It had to be decided what everybody would say in every scenario. It was no use leaving it to the last minute and busking it.

Lee explains: 'It was decided that if we lost to Paris we would say that we had given it our best shot but that we had carried a very important message about problems in world sport. We had been written off early on and yet we had produced a very serious bid. Everybody agreed that if we were asked about another bid in the future, we would answer that there was no decision yet. We would stress that it was a BOA/government decision whether or not London would bid again. Nevertheless, the mood in the delegation was good.

'I was making a conscious effort not to get too excited. Firstly, there was a job to do and I was on duty. Secondly, I did not want to get too carried away because losing would then be a huge blow. Whatever round we might have gone out in, we could always stress that we could not have done a better job but a first-round exit would leave us open to determined attack. Nevertheless the last 72 hours before the vote went the way we wanted it to go as far as the communications and lobbying was concerned. We felt that we had done Britain proud in that respect.'

Lee watched the vote with the rest of the delegation in London's press conference room at the Carlton Hotel. Again Coe decided against joining the large group. He chose to sit with Susie Black in a quiet corner of the hotel bar and ate a very late lunch. It was a wise decision. The atmosphere in the room was extremely tense.

There had been plenty of speculation in the week before the Session that Paris or London could even go out in the first round of voting because there would be so much tactical voting early on. Everybody knew that predicting the way the IOC is going to behave in a host city vote is almost impossible. However, the 2012 vote was always expected to go to four rounds of voting since it was certain that no city would get a majority until three cities had been eliminated.

The system is straightforward. If no city wins a majority of the votes, the city with the fewest votes is eliminated and another round of voting takes place. Although the general view was that New York and Moscow would struggle to survive the first two rounds, both the Russians and the Americans had been working hard to make sure they were not humiliated with single-figure votes. It was widely believed that Moscow had been helped in this regard by Juan Antonio Samaranch, a former ambassador to the Soviet Union, who was keen to make sure his Russian friends were not embarrassed.

The concern for Paris and London was that some of their supporters might feel obliged to vote for Moscow and New York in the first two rounds and the French or British core vote might be squeezed so much that they made an early exit. Paris had been so worried about the prospect that bid Chief Executive Philippe Baudillon had been talking about it in public, effectively encouraging Paris supporters to back the French from the start.

The third round was also expected to be extremely tight between Paris, London and Madrid. The danger for Seb Coe and his team was that London might not even make it to a final showdown.

IOC members were handed their electronic voting boxes. The number of members eligible to vote in each round was different because members from the countries involved were not allowed to take part until their city had been eliminated. Craig Reedie and the Princess Royal sat down at their desk in the ballroom for the vote, hoping never to be handed an electronic box.

The IOC members are not told during an election how many votes each city has received. This is to stop tactical voting. All they are told as every round ends is which city has been eliminated. Sitting in the middle of the top table facing the main body of members, Jacques Rogge made these announcements. The scrutineers, who analysed the electronic results, were led by senior IOC member Thomas Bach, a former German Olympic fencer who had become a successful lawyer and businessman. His job was to look at the result on the computer screen, check the numbers of votes taken added to the members available to vote, print out the result and walk across the room to Rogge. This usually took less than a minute but it made for tense television at the end of each round.

Rogge announced after the first round that Moscow had been eliminated. New York then went out in the second. London 2012 breathed a huge sigh of relief. Now came the crucial third round with Paris, London and Madrid.

London knew their hopes of winning hung on this round. It was an extremely dangerous ballot. London could easily go out at this stage. Even if London went through, there was a serious possibility that Madrid could beat Paris in this round which would be equally damaging to London. It was widely believed that London would struggle to beat the Spanish capital in a final round because more of the Paris voters would switch to support Madrid.

The tension was mounting in both the ballroom and in the Carlton Hotel. There was more drama ahead. The third-round vote had closed, when Lambis Nikolaou, a Greek member who sits on the executive board, suddenly claimed that he missed the vote. The IOC members have two minutes to press the buttons on their boxes but 69-year-old Nikolaou interrupted the meeting, saying, 'I didn't vote, I missed the vote.' Rogge, however, refused to give him a second chance, especially since the members had been given a clear briefing on the voting procedure before the election started.

Lee sat down with his head in his hands as Bach walked slowly over to Rogge with the result. This was the equivalent of a crucial penalty kick in a football game. It was hard to watch. When Rogge announced Madrid had been eliminated the London 2012 delegation in the Carlton Hotel went wild. Lee says: 'There was a real sense in the room that we were in with a very serious chance of winning.'

These few minutes of drama were to cause a huge controversy five months after the election when it was alleged that Nikolaou had mistakenly voted for the wrong city and put Madrid out because the round was so close. But the Greek member denied he had even voted in the round. The IOC confirmed that one member of the 104 members eligible to vote in that round had not managed to register a vote.

Seb Coe was not worried about that on 6 July, however. He was just happy that London had made the final round of voting. Coe says: 'I was relieved that Moscow went out first and then New York, simply because it was the sequence we had expected. But I have to say I never conceived anything but a London–Paris final. I just couldn't see London and Madrid in the final round of voting. It was my gut instinct. For the last four months of the campaign I could not see us not making the final.'

The members then pressed their boxes in the final round between London and Paris. It was a dramatic moment because, although the three scrutineers could see the result, it was not announced to the Session. A card was prepared by the IOC with the name of the winning city and put in a tightly sealed envelope for Rogge to open at 7.46 p.m. Singapore time.

The time had been set by the IOC months before because the announcement was part of a packaged TV programme from the Session which would be broadcast live across the world. The timing was perfect for news bulletins at lunchtime in Europe. It was also a brilliant time for the breakfast news programmes on the east coast of the United States. And in Asia it was prime time.

Few IOC members had a clue which city was going to win, however, in that hour before the announcement. Those who left the room faced questions from reporters. But hardly any of them were ready to call the result with confidence. There was certainly no trend emerging from their comments. It was clear that the 2012 race was living up to its billing as the most competitive race in the history of Olympic bidding.

On the other side of the world, thousands of people were gathering in Trafalgar Square to watch the announcement on a large screen. Many people decided to leave their offices at lunchtime and enjoy the party atmosphere on the square. London 2012 wanted to use the occasion to thank Londoners for their support during the bid. Organisers handed out flags while double Olympic champion Kelly Holmes and former athlete Steve Cram took their places on the stage to talk to the crowd.

At the site of the proposed Olympic Park in Stratford, a group of children and young athletes also gathered to wait for the news. Up and down Britain, people were turning on television sets in bars, cafés and schools to hear the announcement. Drivers switched their car radios on to BBC *Five Live* to listen to the live broadcast. Coe had been right that the campaign had had a 'slow-burn' effect on the British public. Although it took a long time for interest and excitement in the Olympic bid to grow at the start of the campaign, by the time the announcement was just minutes away the nation was fired up about 2012. Many stood in Trafalgar Square in hope, rather than in expectation, however. The belief was that Paris was still the favourite. But London was certainly in with a chance.

On the other side of the English Channel, a similar crowd packed the square in front of the Hôtel de Ville, the City Hall, in Paris. The atmosphere among the youngsters in the crowd was reaching fever pitch. It was incredibly optimistic. There was a real sense that the IOC could not turn their backs on the French for a third time. They felt that it would not be long before Rogge would announce that Paris had won. In the shopping mall attached to the Raffles Hotel complex in Singapore, a crowd of Paris 2012 supporters even began cheering 'Paris, Paris' like football fans. The lobby outside the ballroom looked down on to the mall. The cheering could be clearly heard by IOC members.

Ironically, the man unable to watch the drama unfold was Tony Blair who had played such an important part in the lobbying in the final 48 hours before the vote. Preparing for the G8 summit in Gleneagles, he left his staff huddled around a TV set in the hotel and prepared to take a walk in the gardens with his Chief of Staff Jonathan Powell. Tony Blair explains: 'It was fine at the start because we knew London would do well. I know it sounds feeble but as it got towards the crucial votes, I was that nervous, I had to leave everyone else and go off on my own. By the time it came to the final crucial vote, I went for a walk in the grounds of the hotel with Jonathan.' The Prime Minister made sure he spoke to Seb Coe before the announcement was made, however.

Mike Lee's mobile rang as he was preparing to go into the ballroom; he knew who was on the line and he handed the phone straight to Coe. The bid leader did not have much time before he had to take his place in the ballroom at 7.30 p.m. But this call needed to be answered. The Prime Minister was on the line from Gleneagles. He wished Coe luck and asked: 'Do you think we've got it?'

The bid leader replied: 'I really don't know. It's so close.'

Blair said: 'Yes, I know but what are you hearing?'

Coe said: 'Prime Minister, I really don't know.'

Blair was desperately trying to get a feel for the way the election might go. Coe, like most of the IOC members, simply couldn't call it. Coe says: 'The whole conversation was quite funny really. He was suggesting I must know who had won and I was saying that I simply didn't. It was a bit like that *Fawlty Towers* sketch with me playing Manuel saying, "I know nothing." He was really very nervous. He had played a blinder in the campaign. He had been so good on those one-to-one chats with IOC members. In those situations he is in a different class.'

Tony Blair explains: 'I wish I could say I was saying something inspirational or memorable but it wasn't. I was just telling him what a fantastic job he and the whole team had done, that they had done the very best they could and whatever the result, they should feel immensely proud of their efforts. I knew it was on a knife-edge. I always thought we would have a good chance if the final two cities left were London and Paris, but that it would be more difficult if we were left in with Madrid. Fortunately, we never had to find out.'

But there was no more time for speculation. Mike Lee gestured to Coe that there was just one minute before he had to take his place in the room. Lee was getting worried that the London 2012 chairman was not going to get into the ballroom for the announcement in time. The doors would be shut promptly at 7.30 p.m. because the live TV broadcast was set to begin and nobody would be allowed in once it was live around the world. The rest of the London delegation had taken their seats in the ballroom. But Coe could not simply put the phone down on the Prime Minister.

The chairman eventually told the Prime Minister that the doors were closing and he had to make his way into the room. Blair wished him good luck and at 7.29 p.m. and 15 seconds, the double Olympic champion sneaked through the doors just as they were about to be closed. Lee, who had asked Keith Mills to keep a seat for Coe, pointed to the empty chair and exchanged a look full of emotion with Coe. Coe rushed to the front row. It was another perfectly timed, late burst from a man who had gained a reputation for a devastating kick on the track.

Coe had just taken his seat in the delegation when the TV programme began with videos about Singapore and the bidding cities. In London and Paris, the tension was building dramatically in the crowds at Trafalgar Square and at the Hôtel de Ville. In Gleneagles, Blair was walking slowly around the gardens waiting for the call from Number 10's switchboard. After two years of intense campaigning, the London 2012 team had just sixteen minutes to wait.

Mike Lee had left Coe and made his way to the side of the room. It was then that he noticed that all the photographers were lined up opposite the Paris 2012 delegation. For a moment he was concerned that they might have been tipped off that the French had won and were pointing their lenses at the Paris delegation to shoot the celebration pictures. But, after a moment's reflection, Lee realised that the photographers were probably just taking a punt on the favourites. Nobody else in the room knew who had won, so why would the photographers be any different? Then he started to watch the videos on the screens and the show in front of him, which effectively explained the bidding race in fifteen minutes. As he watched, a strange calm filled his mind and body.

Lee explains: 'Once I was in the room, I could suddenly take stock of the two years of hard campaigning. This was the end of the campaign. We would know in just a quarter of an hour whether all the hard work would result in victory or disappointment. It was a strange emotion I experienced in those fifteen minutes. It was like a single point of light, the emotion was so pure. I took some deep breaths and I felt a Zen type of calm. It was a surreal feeling but, at that moment, the campaign was over and there was simply nothing I or anybody else in the bid could do now. The decision had been taken and we just had to wait.'

On the stage, all the IOC members had taken their place behind Jacques Rogge, who was standing at a lectern sporting the five Olympic rings. The clock was ticking towards 7.46 p.m. and it was time for Rogge to open the envelope with the name of the winning city inside. It was brought to him by a young Singaporean lady in a white dress. The envelope had been placed on a white cushion which had been delicately embroidered with the Olympic rings.

Millions of people watched around the world as the IOC President took the envelope and struggled to open it. Kelly Holmes could not bear to look as she stood on the stage at Trafalgar Square, her head down and her hands clasped together almost in prayer. Steve Cram put his arm around the twice Olympic champion to offer support. Kelly's tension was echoed around Britain in offices, cafés and pubs. For a few minutes, life stopped in most of Britain and France and the nations waited impatiently for the result. Everyone endured an agonising twenty-second wait as Rogge, a former surgeon whose skilled hands have operated on thousands of patients during his medical career, struggled to get his fingers into the envelope.

Lee says: 'It was a very long twenty seconds. There was a real sense of high drama. Everything in the campaign was now coming to a peak. The Zen calm had suddenly gone then from me. The adrenaline was pumping and my heart was beating fast.'

Before walking on to the stage, Rogge had asked his Communications Director Giselle Davies whether he should smile when he made the announcement. It was a difficult decision because the IOC President needed to be seen as neutral in the decision-making progress and a smile might have suggested some sort of bias. On the other hand this was a magical moment for the winner. In the end, Rogge read out the 23 words on the card with no emotion whatsoever. He was absolutely right. It was for others to smile and cheer.

The IOC President said: 'The International Olympic Committee has the honour of announcing that the Games of the Thirtieth Olympiad are awarded to the city of . . . London.' There was a tiny pause before Rogge spoke the final and most important word of the sentence. For a moment in Trafalgar Square and in Singapore, there was a sense of disbelief that he had really said 'London'. Then the reality sank in and the crowd in Trafalgar Square began celebrating wildly. Holmes jumped up into the air and then ran across the stage before finding the arms of Steve Cram. The runner was celebrating with the same joy she had shown when she won her first gold medal at the Athens Olympics. The thousands of people below were waving their flags madly. Many were in tears. Rarely in peacetime have Londoners celebrated together with so much emotion at the heart of the city.

In the Singapore ballroom, the photographers sprinted across the room from the Paris delegation to the London 2012 team. Many focused their lenses on David Beckham who was hugging Steve Redgrave. Everybody in the delegation had jumped to their feet when Rogge reached the end of the sentence and were celebrating his words like a World Cup-winning goal. Culture Secretary Tessa Jowell, Seb Coe, Ken Livingstone, Sports Minister Richard Caborn and Keith Mills were all hugging other members of the London 2012 team with huge grins across their faces.

A few metres away, the Paris 2012 team looked completely dumbstruck and dejected. They could scarcely believe that the IOC members had turned their backs on the French capital for a third consecutive time. It was not long before the tears began.

The news spread rapidly across Britain. Those who missed the announcement on radio or television were told of the news in offices, shops or at the school gate. It was the talk of the country. London's *Evening Standard* held its main afternoon edition back to splash the news on the front page. 'WE'VE WON!' the headline on the front page shouted. In Gleneagles, Tony Blair's garden stroll was interrupted by the ring of Jonathan Powell's mobile phone.

Tony Blair recalls: 'It was Jonathan Powell who told me that we had won. He got a call from our switchboard at Number 10 on his mobile. They had watched the announcement on TV and had been trying to get hold of me, it turns out, to let me know. It was all the more delicious because I think it is fair to say that Jonathan was pretty pessimistic that we could pull it off. As his phone rang, he said: "Here's the bad news". Switch virtually shouted down the phone that we had won. I hugged him, jumped up and down and went on one of those celebratory runs usually reserved for goal-scorers. I'm just glad there were no photographers around.'

Blair considers London's victory one of the high points of his Premiership. The Prime Minister says: 'It was a fantastic feeling, all the better because it was one shared by the whole country. Politics is not like sport. There are not many occasions where the result is absolutely final and you know you have won with no downside or worries and that virtually everyone shares your joy. The fact that it was something of a surprise only made it even better.'

Cherie Blair says the announcement was even more enjoyable than Labour's victory in the 1997 general election. She says: 'At the time of the announcement I was having a massage because we landed and we had a couple of hours before a function. I had watched the presentation on TV and was wishing I was there and then I was told the news. I went to find Tony. I had immense pride and joy at the way everyone had worked together and a feeling that we had actually made a difference. It was just absolutely fantastic and one of the best things that has ever happened to me. In some ways it was better than winning the 1997 election. Tony didn't have any time to enjoy it because he had to go to work immediately. But with this you could really savour it. Then we were waiting for Chirac to come to Gleneagles and were trying not to be too pleased with ourselves. And the Japanese Prime Minister was so funny. There was that whole business about English food and Chirac's comments criticising it, and so every time another course came in at the dinner that night, the Japanese PM would say to Chirac: "This is very good food, isn't it M. Chirac". He was very naughty. To be fair on Chirac, he was perfectly gracious and said congratulations. He is a professional and we had to be professional as well.'

The joy of the Blairs was reflected up and down the country. A nation which has an image for being formal and restrained was celebrating with incredible passion. Car horns tooted, children shrieked and men in suits and ties punched the air in jubilation on the streets. In addition to the jubilation in Trafalgar Square, a large crowd celebrated in Stratford in East London. Confetti showered the crowds at both sites after the announcement was made and champagne was sprayed around under Nelson's Column. Within minutes, jets from the Royal Air Force screamed across the capital's skyline. Trailing red, white and blue smoke the Red Arrows aerobatic team was greeted with renewed cheers. It was a historic moment which Britons will cherish for the rest of their lives. Many will remember where they were when they first heard the news.

In Paris the excited crowd at the Hôtel de Ville was so expecting the IOC President to finish his sentence with the word 'Paris' that they began to cheer at first for a split second before breaking off to issue a collective 'oooh' of disappointment. Many in the crowd could scarcely believe that Paris had not been awarded the Games. A bitterly disappointed Jacques Chirac was preparing to shake hands with Tony Blair at the G8 summit. The French President, however, immediately issued a statement congratulating London and thanking the Paris team for their professionalism.

Thierry Rey, a former French Olympic judo champion, summed up the sense of incredulity. Speaking with tears in his eyes, he said: 'We don't understand. What more could we have done? I wonder if sometimes people don't want us. It was as though we went from forty degrees centigrade to minus two. We took a major body blow.'

A year on, France is still trying to stomach this defeat. There are no plans to bid for the Games again in the foreseeable

future. The details of the vote, released after the announcement, made even more depressing reading for the French.
London led in all but one round of voting. The first round,
London received 22 votes, Paris 21, Madrid 20, New York 19
and Moscow was eliminated with a respectable 15. The second
round saw New York eliminated with 16 votes while Madrid
got 32, London 27 and Paris 25.

London was picking up momentum with every round. But
the third round, where there had been the controversy regard-
ing the failure of Greek member Lambis Nikolaou to vote, was
the closest of all, with Paris just one vote short of a potentially
embarrassing exit. It was in this round that London sowed the
seeds for victory. London won the round with 39 votes, with
Paris on 33 and Madrid going out with 31. If one member,
however, had voted for Madrid instead of Paris both cities
would have had 32 and there would have been another vote
involving all members to decide which of the French and
Spanish capitals would go through to the final round. It is
widely believed that Madrid would have won that 'showdown'
and the favourites would have failed to reach the final round.
Many Olympic insiders believe the Spanish capital would have
certainly made life very difficult for London in the final round
since many Paris supporters would probably have switched to
Madrid. So, if Madrid had picked up one more vote in that
third round, there is a good chance that Spain – not London –
would be hosting the 2012 Olympics.

But this kind of speculation surrounds every Olympic vote.
In the end the reality is that London went on to beat Paris by
54 votes to 50 in the final round.

IOC members stressed that Tony Blair's lobbying in the last
72 hours and the emotional presentation had helped London
pick up the necessary votes which swung the 2012 race in
Britain's favour. Canada's former IOC vice-president Dick
Pound told British journalists: 'You should get down on your
hands and knees and thank your Prime Minister.'

Within minutes of the announcement, Coe was on the phone
to Blair before being escorted by Lee through a series of
interviews with television and radio stations from around the
world. A special news conference was then held in the

ballroom with the IOC to formally hand over the much cherished Host City Contract.

Coe, his assistant Susie Black and Lee then attended a cocktail reception with Jacques Rogge and leading IOC members before heading down to the Indochine waterfront restaurant for an outdoor party organised for London 2012 staff. This party would have taken place had London lost the vote as a way of thanking the staff for their hard work, but, with victory secured, the atmosphere was fantastic. Many of the staff were simply walking around the room hugging their colleagues and laughing and joking. It was not long before the dancing began.

When Coe arrived, the event was taken to another level. The bid chairman was applauded on to the stage where he joined Keith Mills, Ken Livingstone, Tessa Jowell and Richard Caborn for speeches that were cheered to the rafters.

However, it was only when a BBC feed of the news from London was played to the party on a large TV screen that the real significance of the victory sunk in for Coe and his staff. Lee had been shown clips by the BBC team and said, 'Let's show them to the whole party, live at the top of the next BBC World bulletin.' The news pictures had a dramatic effect. Everybody cheered but at the same time, they began to realise the true impact of their work back home. Many had tears in their eyes. Coe says: 'When the announcement was made, there was really no time to think because of all the interviews and everything. It was like winning an Olympic title. As soon as you cross the line, apart from the victory lap, you spend your time giving interviews to the media and having a drug test. You just don't get the opportunity to think about it all. It is only when you go home that you understand what you have done. In Singapore, there were a relatively small number of people involved in the meetings. It was only when I saw the pictures from London from Waterloo Station and Trafalgar Square at the Indochine party and the joy that the victory had brought and also when I got a chance to talk to my kids on the phone, that it all began to sink in.'

Lee agrees: 'My wife and son had been in Trafalgar Square and they told me of the joy, but seeing those pictures helped me really understand what we had done. It was an amazing party and an amazing night.'

Coe finished the night dancing at a night club with Tessa Jowell and other London 2012 staff. Most of the London staff did not get to bed until the early hours of the morning. When they put their heads on the pillows, many of the parties in Britain were just getting going.

Britain has rarely enjoyed such magical moments in the last forty years. The joy at winning the right to stage the Olympics was only to last for a few more hours, however. Less than 24 hours after London and Britain celebrated one of the most momentous events in sporting history, the capital and the country was hit by tragedy.

12. FROM TRIUMPH TO TRAGEDY

B leary eyed and still buzzing from the night before, Mike Lee awoke after less than an hour's sleep and began preparing for another very long day.

London's amazing triumph had sparked the party to end all parties and most of the bid team had not crawled into bed until 6 a.m. or 7 a.m. the next day.

Despite nursing a major hangover Lee went to work. He knew the media's appetite for London's success would be huge. He had to arrange press conferences with all the key figures before a farewell event at Singapore airport. After that there was a long flight through the night to be followed by a celebration, this time on arrival at Heathrow. Whenever Lee's thoughts turned to his bed he simply thought of the moment 12 hours earlier when IOC President Jacques Rogge had declared London the winners and his headache suddenly subsided.

Lee had called a press conference for 10 a.m. at the Carlton Hotel which was supposed to feature the man of the moment Seb Coe alongside Culture Minister Tessa Jowell and Mayor of London Ken Livingstone. The only problem was no one could find Coe.

'We were only ever supposed to have one press conference the following morning after the vote,' Lee says. 'But we had to have two after Seb failed to show up. We needed a little gloss so to avoid embarrassment I told the journalists that we believed that Seb was in a meeting with the Beijing Organising Committee who had asked to see him to congratulate him on London's success. But the truth was we couldn't get hold of him anywhere.'

It all seemed to be working for Lee until Coe eventually showed for the hastily arranged second press conference two hours later.

'The first press conference went really well and Ken and Tessa were on top form and I actually made a bit of a virtue of having a second one with Seb. Despite my initial concerns it was all working out fine. Then Seb comes in and sits down in front of the journalists and says: "As much as I would like to say I've been meeting the Beijing Organising Committee, I am afraid to say I've been in bed sleeping off the excesses of the night before. Sorry." The room just erupted in laughter. Everyone saw the funny side, including me, and Seb went on to give a cracking conference. The morning after London had won, everyone connected with the bid, whether they were part of the bid team or the journalists covering it, were in jubilant mood.'

Within a few hours, however, that mood would be shattered as news filtered through to Singapore of the July 7th terrorist attacks on London. At 3.50 p.m. Singapore time, 8.50 a.m. back in Britain, three suicide bombers began detonating their deadly arsenal of explosives at separate points on the capital's Tube network. The co-ordinated bombings just outside Liverpool Street and Edgware Road stations and another on a train travelling between King's Cross and Russell Square claimed the lives of 39 people. A fourth terrorist detonated his bomb on a bus at Tavistock Place killing 13 people. A total of 700 people were injured as the attack Londoners had long dreaded became a sickening reality.

Suddenly a city which, just a day earlier, had partied at the news of London's triumph, was gripped by fear. Trafalgar Square, scene for the wildest celebrations led by double Olympic champion Kelly Holmes, was deserted as police and ambulance sirens wailed through empty streets.

In Singapore the first sign that something major had happened came when Mayor Ken Livingstone suddenly returned to the lobby of the Stamford Hotel. Livingstone had been shopping when he was told the grim news of events unfolding in London. A group of journalists had gathered around Simon Clegg, the chief executive of the British Olympic Association, when Livingstone pulled him away from the pack.

He whispered something in Clegg's ear which visibly shocked him. Livingstone then walked off sharply across the lobby towards the lifts. Clegg returned to the journalists simply telling them 'there has been an incident but I can't say anything more. Now you'll have to excuse me.'

At this very early stage even Livingstone did not know the full extent of the events unfolding in London. Initial reports suggested the Tube had experienced a power surge which had knocked the network out. Neale Coleman, Livingstone's trusted adviser on the Olympics, had broken the news to the Mayor while he was shopping. He then told Lee what was happening.

'I was actually having a late lunch with some members of the communications team when I got a call from Neale about stories of a power failure on the underground,' explains Lee. 'At the same time I started getting calls from journalists asking for reaction to these reports that London's transport system was breaking down a day after the capital had won the Olympics. It was clear something significant was going on but at this point no one knew exactly what it was or dared to imagine it could be something as terrible as a terrorist attack.

'Various pre-planned media briefings were under way and Tessa Jowell was due to meet with a group of reporters for a chat about the plans for celebrations on our return to London the next day. There was talk of getting a helicopter straight from Heathrow to the site of the Olympic Park at Stratford.

'But while Tessa was doing this briefing, I got an update from Neale Coleman telling me it was almost certainly bombs. In the distance I could see other journalists beginning to get into groups and talking. All sorts of questions were running through my head, not least about the welfare of my own family. I went across to Tessa to tell her of the suspected terrorist attack and that it was important that she gets out of the lobby.

'I then started getting my team together and tried to contact Seb who was up the coast somewhere having lunch with his PA Susie and a few of the team. It was important to brief Seb and protect him from strolling back into the hotel looking relaxed and blissfully unaware of what was happening.

'The IOC were about to have a prearranged press conference so I knew I had to rush and see Giselle Davies, their head of communications. As soon as I arrived at the IOC area, I was ushered straight through to see Jacques Rogge. He and his main adviser were following events on television so I updated them on what I knew at that stage. I knew now from the Mayor's office that there were bombs and scores of people dead. As we discussed these terrible developments the President made it clear that the IOC would stand side by side with London and would make it clear that there was nothing to link this to the Olympic movement or the 2012 decision.

'On a personal level I knew it would be highly unusual for my immediate family to be in central London at the time, but I spent a few minutes trying to reach my wife and son but there was no way you could get through on the mobile because the police were jamming the phone networks. But clearly many members of the team had friends and families who could have been caught up in it. It was an anxious time but I knew we in the communications team had to remain focused.'

As the full extent of what was happening became clear, a mood of helpless desperation and gloom descended on Singapore. Athletes such as Olympic triple jump champion Jonathan Edwards walked through the hotel lobby looking desolate at the way their emotions had gone from one end of the scale to the other in the space of a few hours. Lee adds: 'The hugging that was going on the previous day out of elation and joy turned into people hugging each other out of a sense of horror and fear. Amidst all that was going on there were moments of reflection and your thoughts did go immediately to those who had suffered injury and the families of the bereaved. It was impossible to appreciate the scale of it and how this incredible emotional high had been transformed to the sheer horror and shock of the terrorist attack. It was the most unbelievable change in emotions I have ever experienced.'

Lee knew it would be inappropriate for any of the leading figures on the bid to comment while the picture was still emerging. It was down to Ken Livingstone, as mayor of the city under attack, to take the lead role. Lee says: 'I put up a bit of an iron wall. It was not right that the bid should go beyond expressing our sympathies for the victims and their families and our shock at what had happened. At moments like this, it is right that the political leaders of the country and the city are at the forefront.'

At this point Livingstone rose to that challenge. He called a press conference in the lobby of the Stamford Hotel and delivered an emotional but defiant speech designed to inspire Londoners. It was a deeply moving moment for anyone who saw or heard it.

As a huge pack of journalists and camera crews gathered around him and with his voice trembling with emotion, he said: 'This was not a terrorist attack against the mighty and the powerful. It was not aimed at Presidents or Prime Ministers. It was aimed at ordinary, working-class Londoners, black and white, Muslim and Christian, Hindu and Jew, young and old. It was an indiscriminate attempt to slaughter, irrespective of any considerations for age, for class, for religion. In the days that follow, look at our airports, look at our sea ports and look at our railway stations and, even after your cowardly attack, you will see that people from the rest of Britain, people from around the world will arrive in London to become Londoners and to fulfil their dreams and achieve their potential. This attack isn't an ideology, it isn't even a perverted faith, it is mass murder. But nothing you do, however many of us you kill, will stop that life . . . where freedom is strong and people can live in harmony . . . whatever you do, however many you kill, you will fail.'

Lee recalls: 'It was a magnificent statement. What was so emotional about it was that the same values and strengths of London that were put into the bid, Ken brought out again in a moment of defiance against the terrorists. Ken emphasised the values of tolerance and diversity, the resilience and warmth of Londoners. It was the statement of a man who truly loves London and even though he was incredibly emotional he did keep it together. Afterwards I joined Ken, Neale and the key members of his team in a lift up to his room and away from the cameras we were all in tears.'

Reflecting on the roller-coaster of emotions provided by those two incredible days in Singapore, Livingstone explains how the painful memories of the 7 July bombings will never leave him.

He says: 'The build-up to going to Singapore was very intense. There was so much at stake and very seldom in my life have I been to something where the outcome is uncertain. Everything was to play for and everything had to be done. And London had a wonderful team, everyone was so good.

'Normally in politics everyone is circling like sharks trying to pull down whoever is the leader. But everyone here was buoying up Seb and it was a very uplifting thing to be a part of.

'In parallel with that, one of the biggest aspects of my life has been preparing for the bombings. After 9/11 the government established the resilience committee and we went to these meetings every month examining every aspect. We spent time discussing gruesome details such as where you would accommodate 10,000 bodies, how you would cope with the mortuary needs, where you would take the rubble if Canary Wharf was destroyed. In painstaking detail we had gone into every aspect of how the city would be attacked and what we would do about it. There was never a time when I didn't expect this to happen, I know a lot of people said we were all scaremongering but we really did know from what the police were picking up that one day someone would get through.

'We actually did all the studies of what happened in the Tube blasts and I knew how terrible it was and it is just impossible to think about that without it hurting and I can't imagine it's ever going to stop. What was so important is you had this incredible mood around the people in Singapore, the horror of the 7th and then the wonderful resilience when we got back. Everyone stuck together. We are not aware of any Londoner attacking another and a poll we conducted some time after showed people are more confident about this city than any other time, they are less frightened and they think the communities are working really well. It's an absolutely wonderful city. The reasons for us winning the Olympic Games, specifically the fact that we are the whole world in one city absolutely underpinned what I said in response to the bombings. That makes me immensely proud to have been mayor of this city. And while what happened on the 7 July will always be remembered as a horrific, tragic moment in London's history it was also an amazing moment to be mayor and witness Londoners' resilience to adversity.'

In the hours that followed the bid itself responded as Coe, Jowell and Keith Mills all issued statements expressing sympathy for the victims. 'The entire 2012 team are shocked and deeply saddened by today's tragic events in London,' said Coe. 'Our thoughts are with the families of the bereaved and all of those who have been injured in these despicable terrorist attacks.'

Mills added: 'Even London, that has probably the best and most sophisticated security services in the world, finds it difficult to deal with these sorts of attacks.' Jowell then told reporters that plans to hold celebratory events at Singapore and Heathrow airports had been cancelled. 'It would be inappropriate,' she said.

Back in Britain at the G8 summit at Gleneagles the Prime Minister made the first of a series of statements condemning the bombings, expressing his sympathy for those who had lost loved ones and for the injured and praising the work of the emergency services. 'It's difficult to talk about these two events and two days together,' says the Prime Minister, 'To go from such complete euphoria to shock, horror, and a tremendous feeling of loss and concern for the victims and their families. Worries, too, about what else might happen. In some ways, it wasn't helped that I was up in Gleneagles away from London, playing host to leaders from around the world. Many of their countries, of course, have also suffered dreadfully from terrorism. But you could sense from their reaction just how magnificently they thought London – from our emergency services to millions of ordinary Londoners – had reacted to this

nightmare. And that made me immensely proud to be representing this country.'

The flight back to London from Singapore was due to leave at
midnight and soon the bid team were heading for the airport.
But there was to be another touch of drama before the day was
out. As the team strapped themselves into their seats for the
12-hour journey the British Airways crew suddenly announced
that one of the engines had developed a major fault and they
couldn't take off.

'By this stage everyone was so shattered and desperate to
sleep,' says Lee. 'So we got on the plane and are just settling
down when this announcement was made saying that there
was a major problem with the engine. We were ready to go and
then this happened. It quickly became clear that we were not
going to get away that night. Of course for Ken and Tessa it
was absolutely vital that they got back to London as quickly
as possible so we found out that there were seven places on a
flight leaving at 5 a.m. The key politicians with Seb and
Keith were put on that flight and the rest of the team were
taken back to the hotel to wait 24 hours for another flight.
There was a great sense of desolation as we were filing off
this plane in the early hours of the morning. Given everything
that had happened, a delayed flight home was a mere
inconvenience.'

But for one senior member of the bid team, the wait to get
out of Singapore and back to loved ones in London was even
longer. David Magliano, the marketing director, collapsed
shortly after the IOC vote on 6 July and was taken to hospital
with a kidney stone. He was taken violently ill while waiting
for a bus outside the hotel with Martin Sorrell, chief executive
of advertising giant WPP, and Michael Grade, chairman of the
BBC, who had both travelled to Singapore as part of London's
delegation. Magliano watched the horrific events of the 7 July
bombings unfold on TV from his hospital bed.

He recalls, 'When I turned on the TV and saw what had
happened with the bombings, it was like being punched in the
guts. I was in the airline business at Go during 9/11 so I just
had that terrible feeling of recognition in the pit of my

stomach. Never had I experienced such an extreme swing of emotions.'

Upon his return from Singapore Livingstone held a joint press conference with the Metropolitan Police Commissioner Sir Ian Blair. He told journalists that the reasons London had been chosen as an Olympic host city were also the reasons why London would not be cowed by the terrorists. Insisting he would be travelling to work by Tube on Monday and encouraging the rest of the capital's residents to do the same, he added: 'I say to those who planned this dreadful attack, wherever they are hiding watch next week as we bury and mourn our dead, and watch new people coming to this city to make it their home and call themselves Londoners.'

In the space of 48 hours London had experienced the full range of emotions. Delirious highs followed by desperate fear and horror. But at no point did anyone use the bombings to question whether London was a safe place to stage the world's biggest sports party in 2012. If anything it had made London and Londoners more determined to put on a great show.

13. TOWARD 2012

As London tried to get back to normal in the aftermath of the 7 July blasts and the failed follow-up attacks on 21 July, Lee and the bid team began the task of attempting to meet the challenges of delivering the 2012 Games. An interim London organising committee (LOCOG), chaired by Seb Coe, was established and the process of actually acquiring the land needed for the Olympic Park development stepped up. An Olympics Bill, which would offer statutory protection to advertisers and sponsors to prevent ambush marketing in 2012, had been drafted and had to start its passage through the House of Commons while the preliminary work on venues was started.

At a press conference ten days after the triumph in Singapore, Coe announced London's plans for the first 100 days on the seven-year-long road to the 2012 Games. Lee says: 'It was important that London showed it was moving on and would not be cowed by the attacks. Senior members of the team joined Ken in grieving and signing the book of condolences for the victims of the bombings. At the same time it was crucial that work didn't stop – we were one part of a resilient London.

We were working with the Government and the Mayor to set the course for the road ahead and we had to agree the new structure of the body to deliver the venues, the Olympic

Delivery Authority (ODA). Behind the scenes things were busy. I agreed to stay on and to be a part of the new structure for six months. We mapped out the first 100 days which acknowledged the scale of the task ahead. The task of building the Olympic Park alone is enormous. It will be a complicated process, with complex land assembly issues, land remediation and infrastructure. This is exactly why the ODA has been set up to be separate from the organising committee. This is something previous Games have not done. But for us, the Mayor and the Government it was clear. The ODA would lead in the capital investment and the building of the infrastructure and venues while the LOCOG would be responsible for all that goes into the staging of the month of sport which makes up the Olympic and Paralympic Games. I'm sure that this separation will help make the Games' preparation function much more efficiently and smoothly.'

There can be no doubting London has made an impressive start to the preparations for the Games. Whereas delay characterised the start of the bidding process, the capital has hit the ground running in the race to be ready for 2012. A chairman and chief executive of the ODA was in place by November 2005. The government were keen to hire the best in the business regardless of their nationality. So, American construction industry specialist Jack Lemley, a former chief executive of Transmanche-Link, the consortium of 10 British and French companies responsible for the Channel Tunnel, was appointed chairman. His chief executive is Australian David Higgins, another construction industry specialist, who headed national regeneration agency English Partnerships. He also has experience of delivering Olympic projects, having been chief executive of the Lend Lease Group in Australia, which built the Olympic Village and aquatic centre for the Sydney Games in 2000.

Then, just before Christmas 2005, LOCOG chairman Sebastian Coe announced the appointment of his new chief executive Paul Deighton. With Keith Mills moving up to deputy chairman of the organising committee, Deighton was brought in from Goldman Sachs to run the day-to-day operation which will eventually stage the Games. To use a theatrical analogy, the 49-year-old banker has the task of putting on the show while Lemley and Higgins have to build the stage. To stage that show LOCOG's staff will rise in number from around 65 to more than 3,000, as the myriad venues and stadiums take shape and begin operations. It is also Deighton's responsibility to raise the £2 billion needed for the Games and he, together with Mills, will work to secure that funding in sponsorship, ticketing, IOC television money and the licensing of London-related services and goods. LOCOG will provide the specifications for the venues required to host the 26 sports (softball and baseball were removed from the Olympic programme in Singapore) which will feature in the 2012 Games.

Over the first three years much of the work will take place underground, including the burying of miles of cable currently bringing electrical power into the capital in a massive feat of engineering costing more than £100m. Most of the venue building is not likely to begin before 2008 though the ODA have started a review of costings and venue plans to ensure the Olympic Park is delivered on time.

Speaking at a press conference to mark his appointment, Paul Deighton acknowledged the scale of the opportunity and enormous amount of work ahead and said: 'As a Londoner passionate about sport, I am extremely excited about this opportunity. The Games has an enormous potential to inspire young people. The memories of the Games I listened to and watched in my childhood are some of the most inspirational memories I have. To help stage the Olympic and Paralympic Games, the world's most important sporting and cultural events, in my home city is a dream come true. The London 2012 Games represents an unprecedented and unrepeatable opportunity to combine so many of my professional experiences with my love for sport. Few projects or events have the scope or the impact on a city or its communities and citizens like the Olympic Games. I am delighted to be part of it.'

At the same time as the new leaders of the project were coming on board, so Mike Lee left. After more than two of the most remarkable years of his career he decided to quit to set up his own public relations consultancy called Vero Communications. He was replaced by one of his most trusted lieutenants Jackie Brock-Doyle.

As he reflects on the achievements of the two-year campaign and the promises made in Singapore, Lee is confident the project has made a strong start. But he knows there are many hurdles ahead.

'London won with an exciting mandate but it's not one that London can deliver alone. There needs to be a set of partnerships and alliances that come together under the banner of the London Olympics. That's a huge challenge. It's partly about new sporting venues and facilities but also real sustainable development beyond 2012 in Olympic sport nationally and internationally. These are not easy things to do but the opportunities are unprecedented.

'The next phase has to be focused on developing the new Olympic Park and LOCOG will start on its significant sponsorship programmes. And as long as Seb is there the broader vision that was expressed when London won will be there too – he is the consistent thread with the track record in sport and the voice of the Olympic movement.

'The organising committee will have to grow significantly over the next few years. It will need to evolve as it grows. We excited people with a vision that was the heart of the bid, and for me, the commitment to that vision continues. As much as I enjoyed the first six months as we set up the organising committee it is also time personally for a new challenge. There is much around the build-up to 2012 which I want to be involved in and will stay closely in touch with the whole project. I believe in what we did and I also believe it will be delivered. Whether the full global vision is delivered only time will tell but it's a noble aim and a real opportunity for London, Britain and the Olympic movement.

'We won because we had a real vision for the Games and because we had the support of the British people. We owe so much to the communities of London and to those who worked so hard up and down the country for the bid. Now it is time to deliver for them and for the next generation of young sports people.'

Ken Livingstone, who has said he wants to still be Mayor when the Olympics open in 2012, believes the Games provide a chance to really confirm London as a truly global metropolis. 'Everything is set up around us becoming a more international city with many more people coming from abroad,' he says. 'In terms of economic dynamism we already outrank anything else in Europe by 20 per cent and the next most effective city is Brussels and I think that is distorted by the European Commission. We have made a very good start to the project, we have got a good team in place. David Higgins has the capacity to deliver it on time and as near to budget as we are going to get. I am very optimistic and confident. Honestly, it may not be better than Beijing, no Games will ever be better than Beijing because the money being spent on Beijing is £20 billion. For China this is not just about the Games, it's a statement of the whole future of the world and the role they are going to play in it and no expense has been spared on that. It's more than the Games, it's China emerging as a global superpower.

'We'd be mad to try and match them. After Beijing, people will look at us, and say they didn't spend anything like as much as that but it was a wonderful Games and we might be part of that trend that people keep talking about of scaling the Games down so that more cities and countries can afford it.

'We are certainly doing our best to scale down the spending. I suspect the real problem is we've now got six years of negative press coverage, gloom and woe, doom and gloom, then it will be absolutely brilliant on the day.'

On that note, Lee certainly has some concerns too. 'After a lot of hard work we did create a real mood of support among the British media particularly in the final stages of the campaign, and it is clear that you cannot sustain that so easily when you become an organising committee. The media don't like being in collaborating mode for too long and you are bound to face a much more critical and potentially hostile media, which we dealt with throughout huge chunks of the bid. It now becomes an agenda driven by daily news and there's always bound to be a focus on delays and budgets and people will be looking to find ways of driving different sorts of news angles. That's reality.

'There is a massive challenge to overcome that. Most organising committees find that difficult as, by the very nature of the task, there are bound to be deadlines missed. The key questions you have to ask in all of this are: will it be ready on time and will London host a great Games? And the answer to both questions in my mind is an emphatic yes.

'In communication terms the key will be to try and stay on the front foot. In a bid campaign it's possible to create a rich stream of stories and be proactive. In the seven-year life cycle of an organising committee that's going to be more difficult, particularly in the early years. The danger is if the media and the public don't fully appreciate that this is a seven-year programme.

'People can lose patience and they will, but the gains to sport, UK plc and to the nation's young people should stay on the radar screen. As a country we can rise to the challenge. We have to keep an eye on the final prize and, as the team did with the bid, build momentum. In bid terms it was about winning in Singapore. Now it's about a great Games with a lasting legacy.'

The journey from those early, tentative steps in late 2002 to the joy of 6 July, 2005 and then the tragedy of the following day has been a roller-coaster experience for not just those connected with the bid but for the country as a whole. For so many years, Britain was blighted with a 'can't do culture'. Images from the Sydney Olympics sparked not only delight at British competitors' success but also envy that we hadn't staged an event on that scale since 1948. The Wembley Stadium, Dome and Picketts Lock sagas had left people with a sense that when it came to sport and international grand projects, we were rotting in the second division. The Manchester Commonwealth Games in 2002 began the turnaround and then with one remarkable moment in Singapore the image of a nation was truly changed through sport.

And as the difficult task of preparing for the Games gets under way, everyone connected with the 2012 Olympic project knows it will be a hard slog and there may well be days when it will feel like the wheels are coming off. But Lee knows that's how it felt during the bid too. And as long as people remember the amazing feeling when London won and the opportunities that now lie ahead, then he has no doubt it will be an Olympic and Paralympic Games to make Britain and the world proud.

INDEX